Our Little Secret

Our Little Secret

My Life in the Shadow of Abuse

Tori Dante
with Julia Fisher

Hodder & Stoughton
LONDON SYDNEY AUCKLAND

British Library Cataloguing in Publication Data
A record for this book is available from the British Library

ISBN 0 340 78950 X

Typeset by Avon Dataset Ltd, Bidford-on-Avon, Warks

Printed and bound in Great Britain by
Clays Ltd, St Ives plc

The paper and board used in this paperback are natural recyclable
products made from wood grown in sustainable forests.
The manufacturing processes conform to the environmental
regulations of the country of origin.

Hodder & Stoughton Ltd
A Division of Hodder Headline Ltd
338 Euston Road
London NW1 3BH

Contents

Acknowledgements

I would like to thank Cam, my family, my friends, Altrincham Baptist Church and The Message for supporting me through everything. I would also like to thank those affected by my father for their courage. I am amazed at what they have accomplished in their lives despite everything.

Foreword

When I first met Tori I can remember thinking what a scary person she seemed and despite the fact that she was through her Goth stage she seemed very dark and very angry with the world in general and me in particular.

I think the main reason she was angry with me, and let me know it, was that she blamed me for changing her boyfriend Cameron. The fact that all I did was pray for him and speak to him about my faith, and that it was God who was to blame for the rest didn't quite hit home with her. She wanted back the drug-taking mad-head who she had fallen in love with and she didn't take kindly to me and my attempts to help Cameron to grow in his fledgling faith and to sort his life out.

I can remember the times I would go to their flat in Salford – even though at this point in his life Cameron was earning money from his DJ-ing, they were living in a high rise in one of the toughest parts of town, perhaps because most of their money was being spent on illegal substances. The security man who would escort me to the 9th floor had tattoos on his face and neck and a look that said he ate Christians for breakfast.

What was even worse was that when I got to the flat Tori and their lodger Ian would make clear their disapproval of me and retreat to the kitchen with much huffing and puffing. I had to stay in the lounge with Cameron and an open Bible thinking 'can't someone else do this?'.

However Cameron's hunger for the Bible and passion for Jesus kept me going on and bit by bit it became obvious to Tori and Ian that this was not some little phase he was going through, but that it was for good and that he was actually a better and mucher happier person as a result of it.

I remember well when the penny finally dropped for Tori at Spring Harvest. She had been off at another venue with Cameron and had at last stood up and unreservedly given herself to Jesus. She came into our prayer meeting and announced this to everyone and to my utter amazement gave me a big hug. I had to do a double take because as I looked at her I realised she looked completley different. The hardness had gone and as corny as it sounds she was literally glowing. I jumped for joy on to the dressing room table which promptly collapsed to the floor with a great crash. I had to go and see the venue manager and explain it wasn't our practice to trash dressing rooms, but that it was just that someone who I'd been praying for so much had just become a Christian!

Since then God has been at work big-time in Tori's life dealing gently with all the trauma and pain that you are just about to read about. I do know for sure that she is not the woman she was and that God is slowly but surely transforming her into a real woman of his own.

This disturbing story is one that needs to be written and we all need to sit up and take attention. Hopefully it will help thousands who had suffered similarly and make many turn to the only one who can really heal the pain and, like he has done for Tori, give them a hope and a future.

Andy Hawthorne
The Tribe

1

My darkest night

I was sixteen years old when my father violently raped me, bringing to an end ten years of mental and sexual abuse. We were alone in the house when it happened. My mother, Sheena, was away leading a Guide camp. If I had realised that I was to be on my own with him in the house, I would never have returned home from school that weekend.

After ten years of frequent sexual abuse, I was reaching the age when I no longer felt it necessary to quietly comply with his demanding behaviour. Until now I had managed to survive his assaults by blocking out all thoughts about what he was doing to me; I could, as it were, flick a switch in my head and become totally impassive to him. I suppose it was my way of surviving; I wanted to pretend that it wasn't happening. But for some months now I had become increasingly difficult and argumentative, deliberately trying to annoy him. I was fed up and angry at what he was doing to me – I hated it and wanted him to stop. For years I had felt powerless to do anything but now I was changing; I was not so afraid of him and I was prepared to challenge him.

He was paying a lot of money for my education at a private girls' school – a fact he often used to remind me of. So, one day, I decided to make no further effort with my studies and deliberately appeared to lose interest in my school work. He placed a great deal of importance on education and 'good breeding'. To me, he was a snob; he only wanted to impress people so they thought more highly of him and helped his business prospects. But I had no intention of helping him in the popularity stakes; I wanted to upset him and make people realise he wasn't the respectable, kind father he made himself out to be. I reasoned one way I could get my own back on him was by wasting his money, so I started to look for every excuse to spend. It wasn't difficult. We had a family account with the House of Fraser so, from time to time, I would go on a spending spree taking some of the girls from school with me. I'd tell them each to choose an expensive jumper and then I'd pay for them, using the card. This had a double benefit: not only did it annoy my father, it also made me very popular at school! Other times I would take my friends horse-riding at the weekend. Spending his money became one way I felt I could get back at him. I loathed him, he disgusted me and I hated being with him or being seen with him. I had no respect for him; in fact, I felt ashamed of him and ashamed of being known as his daughter.

When I first had my ears pierced he objected, so I carried on: six in one ear and four in the other! He would tell me not to have any more done, so I would go home with yet another earring in. If he showed any displeasure at my behaviour I was delighted because that indicated how I could annoy him all the more. I started to go out drinking with my friends. We would leave school and go into the town and drink cans of cider, often getting a bit worse for wear and going back to school somewhat 'squiffy'. The school soon realised what we were doing and duly complained to my parents. My dad would tell me off, but I had annoyed him, and that was what I wanted to do – I had succeeded, so I continued drinking. In fact, I went out drinking more often! For years he'd frightened me into submission. But I was changing and it was only a matter of time before the emotional time bomb inside me would explode. Perhaps he was sensing this.

I had gone to bed early that evening having really annoyed him. We had argued. He found my behaviour towards him rude, hostile and challenging. I could tell I had rattled him more than usual and his behaviour towards me was angry. In fact, when I left him to go upstairs, he was in a quiet rage. I was hoping I had annoyed him so much he would leave me alone that night. I started to become a little afraid; I had been even more outspoken than usual . . . never had I answered him back like that before. As I undressed, my fear increased. We were alone in the house. Was I sensing danger? I layered the bedclothes on top of me. Layer after layer after layer. I was hot, yet cold with fear. I pulled the blankets up high around my chin and secured them tightly around me. Surely if I had annoyed him that much he would leave me alone. I lay there in the dark, wishing I had never come home. I listened in case I heard him moving around downstairs. Everywhere was quiet. Time passed slowly, but eventually I must have drifted into sleep.

The sound of him noisily opening my bedroom door woke me with a start. My heart started to beat wildly. I knew something was wrong. Usually he crept in silently, and was on top of me before I knew it. Maybe it was because he had the freedom of the house that he turned on the light and, moving quickly and defiantly, he boldly pulled the blankets off my bed. There was no soft talk tonight. No telling me to lie still while he gave me a 'cuddle'. Before I had a chance to get off the bed, he was on top of me. But the rising tide of fear in me made my reactions fast too. Sensing his anger, my courage rose to match. I don't know to this day where I got the energy from, but I pulled my legs back and put my feet on his chest

3

and pushed him away as hard as I could. He fell backwards, lost his balance and landed on the floor.

My heart was racing. For a moment he was dazed. But looking like a wild animal he came rushing towards me again. Was he going to hit me? Or was he going to do something worse? The resulting humiliation coupled with my challenge to the emotional control he had exerted over me since I had been a little girl sent him into an uncontrollable rage. He grabbed my wrists and dragged me from my bed along the dark landing to his bedroom. Never had I experienced him in such a violent and dangerous mood. He flung me on to the bed and ripped my nightdress off. As I lay on the bed he shouted at me to open my legs and lie still. He wanted to take pornographic photographs of me before continuing with his terror. By now I was shaking with fear. I wanted to run but I was scared of him catching me and then what would he do? I noticed his camera was already set up at the foot of the bed so he had been planning this, knowing we would be alone. He knew exactly what he was wanting to do. This was obviously a premeditated rape.

I refused to co-operate so he violently forced me to open my legs. I was terrified. I fought back. He held a pillow over my head to quieten me. I felt as though I was going to die. I thrashed about, trying to gasp for air. I was petrified. It was hot. I couldn't breathe. He was holding the pillow so tight. I felt faint. I was losing my strength. I stopped struggling. Moving to his camera he shouted at me to open my legs. I heard the camera clicking. My strength started to return and as he stood behind the camera looking through the lens I rolled off the bed and ran to the door. But he had locked it. He caught hold of me again and flung me back on to the bed. I started crying and screaming but he told me there was no point in making a noise – nobody was there to hear me. He put the pillow back over my head and continued. The house was in the middle of nowhere, he knew we would not be disturbed. So I stopped screaming and crying and instead begged him not to carry on. But he wouldn't stop. My stifled cries made no difference. He pushed a vibrator roughly into my vagina before turning me over and thrusting his penis into my anus. The pain was excruciating. My body went rigid with shock – I couldn't move a muscle. All my strength was suddenly gone; instead I was filled with utter panic. Could this really be happening? Could he really be this cruel and hurt me this much? Surely I was about to wake up and find I'd been having a nightmare.

It seemed to last for ever. But eventually he ejaculated, his frenzy ceased and, as usual, he got out his handkerchief and cleaned himself up. I felt him get off me and listened as he made his way to his bathroom. I lay there for a few seconds to make sure he'd really gone. I felt weak and numb with pain and shock. Dragging myself off the bed, half crawling, I made my way to the door. Thankfully the key was still in the lock and I was able to open it and make my agonising way to the bathroom.

I didn't see him again that night. I lay on the bathroom floor for a long time, dazed and bewildered. I felt cold and wrapped myself in towels. My body was shaking uncontrollably. He had obviously hurt me because there was a lot of blood and a lot of diarrhoea. I felt really tired and eventually managed to crawl back to my bed.

And that was it. I didn't visit a doctor, there was no way I'd have been allowed to. In any case, what would I have said? It would have meant making up a story, and how do you make up a story to cover an incident like that?

The next morning we got up as usual and he took me out and bought me another horse, called Pepper. I suppose he thought he'd conquered me. For ten years he'd been sexually abusing me. And for ten years I had tried to ignore what he was doing to me – I suppose I was trying to deny that it was happening. But this rape was the culmination of everything that had gone on before. Maybe he had surprised even himself at the violence he'd shown towards me. I think maybe he frightened himself, because before this happened I was beginning to get mouthy and stand up to him and maybe he was afraid that I would start to speak to my mother, or worse still, the police, and expose him.

He had once taken photographs of my sister, Dianne, boasting in his threatening way that she would not see them until after he'd died. Apparently he'd left them to her in his will. Throughout our childhood, he tried to frighten us by making us afraid of him, forcing us to be silent.

After this rape I really wanted to kill him or, better still, seriously harm him, to pay him back. I was sick and tired of his friends and colleagues telling me what a great guy my dad was. If only they knew! My hatred of him and anger towards him now became the focus of my life. He had tried to destroy me and I was determined to fight back. He was not going to destroy me.

And so, bizarre as it may sound, the next day he took me to see a horse and bought it for me. When my mother came home she was angry to find that I had another horse, because we already had two that weren't being particularly well cared for. I used to love my horses, but as I had grown up, boys had become more interesting. Also, it was another way of annoying my dad and spending his money. It's strange, because I really did love those horses, but because he'd bought them for me I came to see them as payment in kind for his perverted behaviour towards me. So if I showed them love and attention, to me it was a contradiction. I had to disown them and show no interest in them, otherwise he would have thought he could bribe me further. I thought it strange that my mother didn't question him as to why he'd bought Pepper, but as usual nothing more was said. I suppose from his point of view he'd got what he wanted. Perhaps I should have told my mother about the events of the night before, but I didn't. But she did know how much I hated him, I couldn't hide that.

I was numb with shock for a long time; it was three or four months later that I remember feeling really scared that it might happen again. Even a year later, even though he had left me alone for many months, I still felt afraid.

Although he had stopped coming into my bedroom at night, he would often seize the opportunity to squeeze me against a wall and demand a 'proper' kiss. So the sexual harassment continued. His behaviour would make me feel physically sick and I realised more and more what a perverted man he was.

But eventually it dawned on me that he had probably turned his attention on to somebody else. So I did what I'd always done, and kept it all to myself. The effect of this on me was that I started to sleep around, letting myself be abused by other men. I've since come to understand that people who have been sexually abused react in different ways. One reaction to abuse is to avoid sex altogether; another reaction is to become gay; other people choose to become very promiscuous and have lots of sexual partners. I have suffered from a low self-esteem because the only love my father showed me was of a sexual nature. So I grew up with the idea that that's what love is and that's what men expect. I became anorexic for a time. I started taking drugs. Although I allowed men to have sex with me, I didn't trust them to be the father of my children. Little did I realise then that I would end up having four abortions because I did not want to run the risk of any child of mine being abused by their father. I had a very black outlook on life and felt myself becoming increasingly depressed and withdrawn. For me, there seemed to be no meaning to life.

Up until this point nobody knew about what was really going on in my life, not even my mother. My dad had always told me this was 'our little secret'. I had my suspicions that something had happened to other members of my family, but it was to be a while before I found out that my story was also the story of other close members of my family, including my sister, Dianne, not to mention my mother's sister, Elspeth, and my cousin, Karen.

2

Life before birth

My earliest recollections go back to when I was only two or three years old. I have some very happy memories of time I spent with my granny and granddad (my mother's parents). I have always felt very close to them, but never understood why until quite recently, when I learnt from my granny that from the day after I was born until I was three and a half years old I actually lived with them all the time, in their house, and not with my parents.

My mother used to work for my dad in his photography business and apparently, according to my granny, I only went to stay with my parents occasionally, for a weekend visit. My granny told me that she was asked to look after me because my mum went straight back to work immediately after I was born. This makes sense to me now, because I could never understand why it was that I felt such a strong and loving bond with my grandmother. I have always felt far closer to her than to my own mother. She remembers those early days of my life clearly, and once told me about the time the family doctor visited her house to find my granny looking after me. Much to her surprise, the doctor asked how the adoption plans were going! She told me how she was very surprised at this suggestion and asked, 'What adoption plans?' Sensing her shock and ignorance about the matter, the doctor apologised and said he assumed she would have known about the proposal.

So it would seem that right from the start of my life I was going to be put up for adoption, and I have come to the conclusion that it was my father who didn't want me. I also now believe that in order to keep me close by, my mother must have arranged for her mother to look after me as an alternative to adoption. We all lived in Edinburgh so, my granny told me, it was easy for my mother to visit me without my father knowing if and when she wanted to spend some time with me.

I have never spoken to my parents about this stage of my life, not even my mother. Looking at it from my dad's point of view, he already had three children from his first marriage, and he wasn't married to my mum when I was born; they were just living together. In fact they had only been living together for three months when I was born.

Even then he must have been a very controlling person. But, according to other members of my family who knew them in those days, my mother was deeply in love with him and would do anything to please him – she just did everything he asked. I am sure my mother loved me, but what he said went. My gran told me how she, as well as my father's family, wanted my mum to leave him and stay at home with her parents; but she wouldn't, and went to live with him after he left his first wife.

Apparently my father's sister, Josephine, once indicated that she would have liked to adopt me. So I have come to the opinion that adoption was openly discussed by the family, and maybe my father would have favoured his sister adopting me just to keep me in his side of the family. There's a part of me that would like to know what actually happened.

I sometimes wonder whether my dad tried to persuade my mum to have an abortion, because I am so sure that he really didn't want me. If my mum refused to have an abortion and my dad refused to have me living with them, then the only option was for me to go and live with someone else. I like to think that my mother loved me enough to want me as close to her as possible so that she could visit me. But one thing is certain: I was an inconvenient baby, and those early days in the womb were dangerous; my life could so easily have been snuffed out. I look back on those days and wonder just how much tension surrounded my tiny life then. If we are affected emotionally by our time in the womb, as some would suggest, then just imagine how much damage occurred to me before I was even born!

So from my dad's point of view I was a major inconvenience. He already had three children and was 'just' having an affair with his assistant (my mum, who was twelve years younger than him) and I am sure he never imagined that he would be faced with the prospect of being the father of a child born as the result of a casual affair. From what I've been told, this was not the first affair he had succumbed to; he was a man of experience and was not used to being caught out by an unwanted pregnancy. After all, from his point of view he needed my mum to help him with his business rather than be at home looking after a baby. Suddenly he was confronted with the problem of his mistress being pregnant with his child. Things could not remain as they were unless my mother agreed to an abortion. But clearly my mother wanted to keep both my father and me. I think she took a big gamble in using me as a bargaining tool, to prise him away from his first wife and establish their relationship. But it worked, and she got her way.

As for my parents, my father was born Reginald John Forester Smith on 30 December 1931 in Cardiff to Josephine and Jack Smith. The family later moved to Weston-super-

Mare, perhaps to get away from Josephine's family, who considered her to have married beneath herself. Jack Smith was an alcoholic and, the story goes, he used to bring waitresses back to the marital home to stay the night. I was told by my mother that Jack had reputedly abused his daughters, who were called Josephine and Barbara, even breaking the nose of one of them on one occasion, although my Aunt Josephine denies this happened to her or to anyone else.

As for my dad, Reginald, he was in trouble with the law even at the age of thirteen, when he was caught breaking into houses. He was tried in court and sent to a remand school for boys, where he met a clergyman who took an interest in trying to help this young lad and arranged an apprenticeship for him with an engineering company.

From there, he joined the Royal Air Force and was stationed in Egypt, where he worked as an aerial photographer taking pictures for cartographers, enabling them to create accurate maps of the area.

Meanwhile, back in Weston-super-Mare, Jack Smith either left home voluntarily or was thrown out and the family changed their name to Shutte (Josephine's maiden name). Reginald's mother signed herself into a home when he was fourteen years old, never to emerge. I met her once when she was a frail old woman who just wanted peace and quiet; by the time I met her she was quite unable to cope with life outside her institution. Reginald's sisters, Josephine and Barbara, also moved away and found jobs as nannies.

In 1953, while still in Egypt, my father met his first wife, who was in the Women's Royal Air Force. They married in 1954 and moved to Edinburgh. At this time he added Forester to his surname to become Forester-Smith. Their first son was born in 1956, followed by Dianne in 1958 and their second son in 1964. It would appear that Reginald always aspired to be someone he was not, at one time leading the family to believe that we were related to Lady

Jane Grey. We even have a family crest!

It was during this time that Reginald opened a photographic shop, where he managed to achieve some modicum of success. He was also very interested in motor racing and enjoyed mixing with racing drivers. He made a category B film in 1967, called *The Racing Driver*, which was shown in cinemas before the main feature, and took several portraits of famous Grand Prix champions such as Jackie Stewart, Graham Hill and James Hunt. He became a member of the Edinburgh Merchant Company and took portraits of many important and influential people who visited the city, including the Queen.

My mother, Sheena, on the other hand, was born into a happy working-class family in Edinburgh on 20 August 1944. Her mother, Elizabeth, was married to Robert McDonald, and Sheena was born the third of four children. Robert, who did not enjoy good health, worked for British Rail, and Elizabeth was employed by John Menzies when they met, although she worked as a chef in a couple of hotels in Edinburgh in later years. Of my mother's two brothers, Robert played football for Hearts of Midlothian, Queen of the South and Notts Forest before he got married, and Derek joined the army after having had a promising early career in cycling. My mother's younger sister, Elspeth, has always worked with horses and was a riding instructor and later a lecturer and examiner. She has worked with race horses and Olympic horses, had her own riding school and taught actors to ride. I think my love of horses comes from Elspeth.

As for how she met my father, Mum worked in a jeweller's shop where she met a man who sold cameras. He knew my father and heard he was looking for an assistant for his photographic shop. One thing led to another, and before long my mother was working for my father.

It was my sister, Dianne, who provided me with an insight into my father's life before he met my mother.

Dianne was born in 1958, the second of Reginald's children. She told me how most of her childhood memories are unhappy ones. She grew up in a respectable area of Edinburgh at Parkgrove Gardens with her mother and father and two brothers. They later referred to the house as 'Parkgrove'.

Dianne told me that she could never remember my father being a violent person, but always remembers feeling very frightened of him. She would never dare talk back to him, just like the rest of us. We all had a very formal relationship with him in those early days.

She remembered most about the time after her younger brother was born; she was almost six years old by then, and she recalled how life assumed a daily routine during the next two years. She and her brothers would get up each weekday morning and get themselves ready for school. Her mother and father argued a lot and on some occasions they shouted and threw dishes at each other. She remembered one such morning kneeling down on the dining-room floor, leaning on a chair with her head in her hands, crying her heart out. My father got angry and shouted at her and told her to stop crying. I could identify with Dianne's story – I never saw him show anybody any sympathy. After he had taken the three of them to school, Dianne told me, they usually didn't see him again until breakfast time the following morning.

His hobby was motor racing. He used to race at Ingliston, just outside Edinburgh, and in the south at Croft. My brothers and Dianne were taken to motor-racing events at Ingliston during the summer months. And it was around this time that, unbeknown to any of them, my father started having an affair with my mother, Sheena. When he didn't go home to them in the evenings, it was because he was with my mother. They later found out that he also took her away for occasional weekends when he was racing at Croft, which I remember my mother telling me about. Apparently he would sign them into a hotel as Mr and Mrs Smith; hardly any of the racing drivers knew his first wife, so he obviously thought he was safe from gossip.

Dianne told me how my father would always be at home with his family for a traditional Sunday lunch. I too remember Sunday dinners: they were always eaten in the dining room and were very formal occasions. My father always felt the need to comment on how we should or shouldn't eat our food. We were told we should put our knives and forks down while we had food in our mouths. After finishing our meal we were not allowed to leave the table until our father gave us permission. I remember having to sit through a music programme which was on Radio 2 every Sunday evening before he would even consider dismissing us. Dianne told me it was just the same for them.

When Dianne was eight years old, her elder brother was sent to St Mary's Boarding School in Melrose. Her parents argued frequently, and although she didn't realise it at the time, it was probably because her mother had found out about Sheena. Dianne recalled how one afternoon after school her father was waiting for her outside the school gates, in his car. He had a lady with him whom he introduced as Sheena. Dianne remembered that Sheena was wearing a cerise pink dress and coat and that she gave her a bag of sweets. Dianne was quite unaware, at that time, that Sheena was pregnant with me.

Then the inevitable happened when, one evening in November 1967, my father's first wife gave him an ultimatum – either finish with Sheena or leave the family home. He decided to leave and moved with my mother to a caravan at Port Seton in East Lothian. On 2 January 1968 I was born.

I was so interested to hear Dianne's recollections of that time. She told me how, six months after I was born, in July 1968, her mum agreed that she and her younger brother could go on holiday with Sheena, Dad and me. Obviously I cannot remember this myself but I have seen the cine film of that holiday. We went to Ireland. My dad hired a gypsy caravan which was pulled by a huge horse called Clearboy. He also had a smaller horse called Charlie. My Aunt Elspeth, who was seventeen at the time, came along with us. Being used to working with horses, she gave everyone riding lessons. We had a lovely time touring through Ireland and stopping off at different caravan sites. The one memorable thing about that holiday for Dianne was that it was free of abuse; there were so many of us sleeping in such a confined space that it was just impossible for my father to do anything to her. By this time she had experienced several years of regular sexual abuse by her father, in just the same way as I was to, a few years later.

Shortly after this holiday, my father moved his new family into a flat in Haddington Place which occupied two floors. The living accommodation was on the ground floor and my father converted the basement into photographic rooms and a studio for his business. Dianne told me how she remembers visiting at weekends and would sleep downstairs in the studio. The studio itself comprised a fairly large room, with a small room leading off it. She slept in the large room and her younger brother slept in the small room. It was in this room that my father abused her. He used to wait until she had been in bed for a while and then creep silently into her room. As time went on and she got a little older she used to try and stop him and struggle with him. Then, she told me, he would get angry with her and shake her and tell her to behave herself. In the end, Dianne told me, it was easier just to lie there – it was over sooner that way.

For Dianne at this time, things quickly went from bad to worse. She told me about one afternoon when my mother was out shopping. My father took her into the front lounge. He laid her on the chaise longue and lay on top of her; she was eleven years old. Her younger brother, who was only five at the time, came through the door. My father jumped up and yelled at him and told him he should never walk into a room without knocking first. A few weeks later he said to her, 'Why was Daddy lying on top of you?' Dianne told him he must have been mistaken and quickly changed the subject.

Dianne said to me once, 'I was very frightened about anyone finding out about what my father was doing to me. He had a way of making me believe that I was being very bad and that I would get into a lot of trouble if anyone found out. I was also aware of how it could upset my mother and Sheena and so, because of this, a very heavy burden was put on my shoulders from an early age.' Dianne was abused into her teenage years.

We were talking one day when she told me, 'On one occasion my father made us bend over and he hit us with a wooden spoon while Sheena stood and watched. On another occasion, when I returned home after a weekend visit, my mother was very concerned about my behaviour. I was obviously extremely upset and wouldn't eat or speak to her. When she asked my father why I had come home in such a state, he told her it was her fault for asking too many questions. These episodes of not eating and becoming very listless and depressed would occur approximately four or five times a year and continued as I grew older.'

As I listened to Dianne recount her story, I could hardly believe what I was hearing, yet it all sounded so horribly familiar. Dianne has written a detailed account of her memories to help her come to terms with her experience; for her, it's been a type of therapy. She allowed me to read her diary, and my heart nearly stopped when I reached the following entry.

On 30 November 1971 my father collected me from Parkgrove and took me to Haddington Place. I am able to recall the exact date; I was thirteen years old and it was St Andrew's Night. I know it was St Andrew's Night because Sheena, her sister Elspeth and her two sisters-in-law were at a St Andrew's Night function. I don't remember anything about going through the door of Haddington Place that evening or leaving to be taken home again. What I do remember, though, is lying in his and Sheena's bed. There was a large mirror on the wall behind the bed where normally there would be a headboard. My father had removed his and my clothing and was lying on top of me, saying, 'I'm going to do it properly to you now' . . . I can still remember the excruciating pain. I screamed and asked him to stop but he just kept saying over and over again, 'It'll be all right, it'll be all right.' After that dreadful night the abuse continued, and each time he came to my room at night he had full sexual intercourse with me.

I was shocked to read Dianne's story: to think that while I was a very young girl and he was doing this to my sister, at the same time he was starting to abuse me.

3

The rape of innocence

I vaguely remember Haddington Place. I was about three and a half years old when I went to live there in 1971 with my parents, leaving my granny's home for good. My memories are of it being a really big house where my dad had a shop. The shop was at the front of the house, and the basement incorporated some living quarters. Behind the basement was the developing area for the photographic studio, and at the back of the house were more living quarters. It was part of a huge tenement block of flats, very spacious, but to me a frightening place. Maybe I found it scary because it was so dark, or maybe I had that sixth sense that things weren't right. I remember being very wary of my dad; I found him frightening too, so I was always quiet when he was around, and I was always aware that he was watching what I was doing.

I remember being terrified of going to bed. When I was very young I slept in a cot with white bars next to my parents' bed. Then I was moved into my own bedroom, a small room downstairs. Beyond my bedroom door was a dark hallway with

19

a dim light that cast an eerie shadow through the half-closed door.

I remember my brothers and sister visiting us quite often. Many of their visits were shrouded in bad temper and anxiety. One vivid memory I have is of walking through the hallway into the kitchen where I saw my older brother crouching on the floor. Next to him stood my mum, threatening him with a wooden spoon in her hand. I remember seeing more of my older brother than my other brother or my sister, Dianne. To me at that time, I felt like an only child with brothers and a sister popping in from time to time. But that's all I knew. I had no idea how other families conducted their lives, so it seemed perfectly normal to have my brothers and sister living in another house.

In 1973, when I was five years old, we moved to West Calder in West Lothian. I remember Wednesday evenings there were fantastic, because my dad went out to some regular commitment in the town. I've no idea where he went, but it was enough to know that there was one evening in the week that Mum and I could relax together. On those evenings, Mum and I would go to the chip shop, then sit in front of the television watching programmes that we weren't allowed to watch when my dad was at home, programmes like *Mash* and *Butterflies*. I used to tease my mum that she was a bit like Wendy Craig except she couldn't cook as well! They were memorable nights, and nights I really looked forward to.

Now that I'm piecing this whole sorry story together, I can imagine how Dianne must have dreaded those nights when her mother would be out and she would be at the mercy of her father. There must have been a sense of inevitability about those evenings for Dianne. Poor Dianne, I sometimes feel more for her than I do for myself. It's strange, thinking back, but I blocked out so much of the pain and degradation of my own experience that, superficially, I hardly feel any pain for myself. But for Dianne and others in the family, I feel great sorrow, and a sense of anger and hostility towards my father for what he did to them. If only we had discovered what was going on earlier. To think he was having his way with each of us in turn, and able to keep it all a secret for so many years.

I remember there were a lot of arguments between my parents at that time, mostly about the other three children or his first wife. I remember one particularly noisy row which started after my dad stayed out overnight. I was aware that there was something going on – he was seeing his first wife a lot and this did cause arguments. Also, I knew that if my brothers and sister came for the weekend there would be arguments, either then or a couple of days later. Dianne didn't come very often at weekends, she had her own friends, but my brothers often came and we were starting to get to know each other quite well. Many of the arguments were sparked by my mother not wanting his first wife knowing what was going on in our house – but, of course, this sort of curiosity and intrigue was impossible to stop. Their mother questioned her three children each time they returned home after a visit to see us, and they would tell her about the new settee and where they had been. For years there were rows between his first wife and my mum, often involving my father's money, although happily they eventually stopped.

When I was very young my father's business went from strength to strength. He opened three photographic shops in Edinburgh, one of which sold jewellery as well. He was successful and very well known, especially by those people who were married in the 1970s and for whom he took wedding photographs.

From the outside looking in, I can understand how he managed to impress people. He had a presence, a flamboyance. He was slightly eccentric, which seemed to attract people to him, especially women; many seemed to enjoy the attention he gave them. When he walked into a room he was noticed. He carried himself well. He spoke well. He was intelligent and had a good feel for business. Women flocked to him. He would dominate a conversation and was always captivating and extravagant. If you went out for the night with him he wouldn't just buy you one drink, he would buy you every drink that night – and he'd pay for the meal as well! We used to go with him to business conferences and sales weekends, and if there was an auction for charity he'd bid for the top prize, maybe a television, then he'd put it back into the auction for it to be sold again. All this made him look generous in the eyes of his acquaintances. His customers thought he was great – a bit eccentric maybe, but very charismatic. To anybody outside of the immediate family, he was a lovely guy, a great buddy and friend.

However, if anybody crossed his path in business or contradicted him in public, they would know about it sooner or later. There was no saying sorry; rather, he would bear a grudge.

At home he made his presence felt but in a different, quieter, more controlling way. He had his own chair in the house so you wouldn't sit there if he was around. But if you were sitting there and he came into the room you had to move. He would put his drink next to you and look at you. He had this stare which affected us all, even my mother. He would pull his glasses down his nose and look over the top of them at you, and your blood would run cold. He wasn't that physical, he didn't particularly batter us, but to me he looked evil and could reduce any one of us to silence. He was the same with his staff. There was just something about him you didn't cross. We all lived in fear of him, and I think he liked it that way.

My father always bought big houses. He also started selling second-hand cars from an empty piece of ground opposite the house. He built a transporter for the cars, and at weekends he would use it for his racing car. Then he sold his first transporter, so he built another one! In fact, he built quite a few after that; it became quite a profitable sideline.

It was at this time that I started to go to Parkhead Primary

School. By now my mum had stopped working for Dad in the shop and stayed at home to look after her family.

The house in West Calder was on three floors, and on the top floor were three bedrooms. My parents shared one, I shared another with my sister when she came to stay, and the third was used mainly by one of my brothers, who was in the army by this time.

My earliest memory of my father abusing me is of around this time in 1974. I woke up in my bed to find my father kneeling over me with his penis in his hands, pushing it down towards my mouth. He held it very close to my lips, asking me repeatedly to kiss it. I said no and kept on turning my head away. I did not understand what was happening, I had never seen a penis before. I knew I did not like what was going on. I was really scared. I have since been asked if this was the first time that anything of this nature had occurred. I can't explain it clearly, but I feel that this was not the first time. I was always frightened of my father, and even though I was scared of what I was being asked to do, it was not a total shock. Somehow, being woken up by my father felt familiar.

I don't remember crying. It finished. He went. I didn't understand what had happened. The next morning nothing was said to me and I didn't say anything to anybody, not even my mother. Our usual morning pattern of behaviour didn't change. I got up as usual to go to school. My dad got up and cooked me a boiled egg as he did every morning and insisted I ate every bit of it (even though I hated boiled eggs!). Sometimes he would give me some money to spend on the way to school, because I always walked to school via a local shop. This was our ritual. Mum never got me up; whether it was because she was a bad sleeper I don't know, but Dad got up and made me my breakfast right through to my time at senior school.

It is very hard to say when the next incident occurred. I remember changing bedrooms all the time. I would move to the room near my mother, thinking that if I was close to her he would not risk it. I remember sharing rooms with my sister Dianne when she came to stay with us. But it didn't matter which room I was in, he always came in. How often he came is hard to say; it felt like every night at one stage. At other times it would be once a week, and on occasions it seemed to stop for a while, for a couple of weeks maybe. But it always started again. When he came into my room it would always be at night after I had gone to bed. He would usually be dressed in his day clothes, but sometimes in his pyjamas. I am not sure what time in the night he came in. It felt really late sometimes, yet at other times if felt as though I hadn't been asleep very long at all.

He always followed the same pattern of behaviour; he would open my bedroom door slowly, and with the light still off he would make his way to my bed. He usually knelt down next to my pillow. Sometimes he would speak and say, 'Okay, I just want a cuddle.' At other times he would say nothing and put his hand under the blankets and touch me. He would first touch my leg and then he would touch my vagina. When he inserted his fingers he would ask me to push so they would go in further. I would just lie there. He would feel my body with his hands, moving them up and down my body. He would touch my breasts. Sometimes he would lie next to me on the bed and insert his fingers into my vagina and ask me to push on them. I remember doing this on many occasions, thinking that, if I did, it would be over more quickly. It never seemed to be.

He would ask me, 'Is that nice?' I would always reply no, and tell him he was hurting me.

He would sometimes lie next to me and get his penis out. He would ask me to hold it. When I refused he would force my hand on to it, asking me to move my hand up and down on it. I would do this a couple of times then refuse to carry on, saying I didn't want to.

He used to tell me this was natural and that all fathers did this to their daughters. He would say he was 'breaking me in'. Whenever I said I would tell Mum, he would tell me that she already knew.

At other times he would lie next to me, touching my body and masturbating himself.

He would try to kiss me with his mouth open asking for a proper kiss. I would keep my mouth shut.

Nothing was ever said the next morning, but I would be given extra pocket money to spend on the way to school. I knew why he gave it to me. He knew why he had given it to me. I was too young then to work this out for myself and realise his behaviour towards me was bizarre. I still had no idea that his behaviour towards me was anything unusual. I believed him when he told me that all fathers did this to their daughters. I suppose I must have thought it was part of growing up. So, to me, sexual abuse was a normal and expected part of my life. It was, quite literally, our little secret.

While I lived in that house, I remember, I was always terrified of going to bed. When nine o'clock came I would get knots in my stomach. Sometimes I still do to this day. If I hear certain theme tunes on television I still get anxious. Programmes like *The Rockford Files,* or *The Sweeney,* or *Panorama*, in those days all started at nine o'clock, and I knew that any time after they had finished he would come up the stairs. When I was in my bed at night I would have recurring nightmares. When I needed to go to the toilet I would be too frightened to get up and go to the bathroom in case I met my father on the landing. So instead I wet the bed or sometimes even wet the carpet. I would turn my toys round to face the wall so they could not see me, especially the ones he had given me, because I was convinced he could watch me through their eyes. Unless I turned them towards the wall, I imagined their eyes followed my every move.

Sometimes in the night I would creep out of my bedroom and go and wake my mum and ask to get into bed with her because I was so scared. She would let me, but he would get really angry with her. On occasions he would insist that I slept between them. Then he would try to cuddle me.

Even though I didn't like what he was doing to me and knew instinctively that the abuse was wrong and it was horrible, I was in a dilemma because he said it was all right. I was young, he was my father and I did what he told me to do. I was brought up to trust him and treat him with respect, so I did what he said, even if I didn't like it.

But little by little, as I grew older, I had a suspicion that maybe my father was different to other fathers, and I had to find out the truth. So, one day, when I was about seven or eight years old I plucked up the courage and told my friend that my dad came into my room at night and was 'breaking me in'. She looked at me really strangely and asked what I meant. I panicked and replied that it didn't matter, and changed the subject. But that was when I realised it didn't happen in every house, even though my dad kept telling me it did. So I decided to keep quiet. Dad told me Mum knew; he said that it happens all the time but you just don't talk about it. I was brought up to respect adults because they tell the truth, and you don't question them because they know best; so I decided there was no point in saying anything to anybody because nobody would believe me. I therefore had to find a way of dealing with this on my own.

I hated my father. I fantasised about finding out whether I was adopted. I didn't want my dad to be my real dad. Every night I had to sleep with layers of covers on top of me as I thought it would make it more difficult for him to get his hands near me. I slept on my stomach with my arms underneath the covers to protect myself. I would get a feeling of suffocation at times. I would lie in the dark and it would seem as if a wall was close, almost touching my nose. But the next moment it would be miles away and I would feel so small. The funny thing was that, even in the dark, sometimes the cover was white – brilliant white, like sunshine on snow. The only other time I have felt this sensation of brilliant white is in prayer. It's almost as if the devil was present one minute and then the light took over and God was there with me.

When Dianne came to stay we would share a bedroom. We realise now that both of us enjoyed sharing a room because we didn't want to be on our own; we were unwittingly using each other out of a sense of wanting some protection, even though we didn't know at the time that we were both being abused by our father.

I can also remember, even though I was so young, being very aware of what sex was and wondering why my five- or six-year-old boyfriend wasn't wanting to have sex with me like my dad.

So my life was a crazy mixture of normality one minute and abuse the next. There were times when Dad would read me a bedtime story, be very normal, kiss me good night – and then four hours later would come into my bed and abuse me.

Looking back, I can now see how my sister and I and other members of the family all behaved normally, even though we were scared of him. We were told to keep our father happy. We knew no better. This was the norm.

I wanted to tell people but I didn't know how. I didn't have the words to explain. He used words like 'cuddle' and 'proper kiss'. But if I had said to anybody that my dad cuddles me, who would think that was strange?

4

The start of resistance

We moved from West Calder to a house called Luce, in Dumfriesshire, in November 1979. I was almost twelve years old. By now my dad had closed his shops in Edinburgh to concentrate on building car transporters; he had acquired a factory in Blackburn, near West Calder, and in addition he was working as a freelance photographer.

Luce was a large mansion, a former dower house. There were two other houses on the estate, which came with 24 acres of land. I had been promised a horse when we moved, and that I could choose my own bedroom. We went to see it on a Friday, and by the following Wednesday my father had bought it. Apparently the previous owner was bankrupt and desperate to sell, so my father bought it for a very reasonable price.

I thought the house was great. I had always wanted to live in a really big house so this was quite exciting for us. I chose my room and settled in. I had the room along the landing from my parents.

For a few weeks, my father seemed to be away for much of the time. We later discovered that he was having an affair with his secretary. However, this was short-lived, and when he returned the abuse continued. Nothing had changed. If anything, it seemed to be more frequent. He was more forceful. He would not give up easily. It followed the same pattern; he would start by kneeling beside my bed; he would masturbate more often in front of me, and then he'd start to rub his penis between my legs, not inserting it, but rubbing it against the very top of my thighs so it would touch my vagina. He would be lying on top of me and pushing down and asking me to push back. I couldn't do it. I found his behaviour extremely upsetting, and when he was doing this to me I would be crying most of the time.

Sometimes he would come into my room during the day, especially after I'd had a bath. But he would just say sorry, and leave. It was as though he was trying to catch me dressing.

If he passed me in the hallway he would grab me and pull me towards him and ask for a cuddle. I would pull away.

In the living room at night he would ask me to sit on his knee and tell me how much he loved me, and he would ask if I loved him. Always, he seemed to be increasing in intensity. Things were not even staying as they were: he was gradually becoming more and more forceful in his behaviour towards me.

After a short time of living at Luce, I realised how much I missed my friends in West Calder. I had made some good friends at the school there and we had been talking about moving on to high school together the following year. I had wanted to do that; I really enjoyed my school life in West Calder.

Mum hadn't wanted to leave either. Apparently Dad would have preferred to move us all to England, but Mum had put her foot down at this suggestion and said she wasn't going to leave Scotland because we were Scottish. My mother had been heavily involved in politics before she met my father; she was a member of the Scottish National Party. And she had been an active member! She was a friend of Wendy Woods, the great Scottish activist who founded the SNP movement. In her younger days, my mother had been known to climb up flag-poles and take the Union Jack down and replace it with the Rampant Lion. She was very vocal about what she believed and would often stand on a soapbox and preach home rule for Scotland at Speakers' Corner on Princess Street in Edinburgh. Every time she heard the national anthem played, she would sit down in protest. She has helped to remove the English sign near Berwick umpteen times!

However, when she married my father he insisted that she leave the SNP and stand up when the national anthem was played. So she relinquished any political ambition she may have had in order to marry him; in fact, she gave up a lot to be with him and, I think, lost a lot of her identity in the process. But he was forever keen to better the name of the family and improve his contacts and standing in the eyes of local digni-taries and business people as well as national political leaders. He often used to write to John Major and, before him, Margaret Thatcher. So my mother, taking such a strong political stance in the way she was, would in time prove damaging to his reputation and his chances of social better-ment. Her activities had to be curtailed.

I am told her family warned my mother about getting involved with Dad. But she was obviously a strong-minded young woman, and it must have been clear that she had made up her mind. So she moved from being a strong independent woman with her own views and beliefs. When she fell in love with him she fell in love with the boss, the high flyer with shops in Edinburgh, the racing-car driver. He beguiled her, swept her off her feet. Speaking to my gran and my auntie, I can see that her whole life changed completely when she met Dad. She idolised him so much he became the centre of her life. They warned her about getting involved with a married man. They warned her to be wary of him. But she rebelled against her family. I suppose if she had gone back home, she would have had to admit she was wrong, and she couldn't do that.

I have been told by my uncle and aunt that my mother was a very compassionate person in those early days. If there was a cause to be fought, she would fight it. Whether the cause was home rule for Scotland or helping waifs and strays, she was there to defend people.

She was also involved in the Brownie and Guide movement, becoming a commissioner, and in fact has continued with that work throughout her married life.

So quite why my father chose to move us to Luce I am not entirely sure. In retrospect the family believe it was to take us further away from them so that he could isolate us all the more. We moved in the November, so I went to the local primary school to finish primary 7. Academically they were a term behind compared with the school I'd attended in West Calder, so I had to repeat much of the work, which I found tedious. The school was half a mile away in a very small village called Brydekirk, which had a population of about 300 people. In Brydekirk there was one shop, one church, one pub and two bus stops! There were three classes in the school, and because there were so few children, despite the wide age range we were often all grouped together. I found having to repeat work I'd already learnt discouraging. When I told my teacher that I'd already covered much of the work, she allowed me to go home! So it was part-time school for me in those days. It felt very relaxed and I had no challenge to work there – so I didn't. The people were very pleasant and very kind. There was no sense of urgency; if the man came to read the school meters, it was not uncommon for us to be given an extended break or even be sent home early!

During these early days of life at Luce, my father was still working in Blackburn, West Calder. The intention was to move the factory to Luce by building another factory in the grounds of the house. But meanwhile he was commuting up and down, staying in West Calder for a couple of nights and then coming home for a night.

During this time the abuse continued, if anything becoming more regular. By this stage he was also drinking quite a lot, almost a bottle of whisky a day. This made him more aggressive and his moods became erratic. During the day he would be the distant, normal father I was accustomed to. He was usually home by six o'clock and would like a glass of whisky next to him. He would sit in his chair, smoking a cigar, and watch the evening news on television before getting up to make some telephone calls. When he was in his office making phone calls he would like his dinner to be prepared. When we first moved to Luce we would all sit down at the table together, but when he started coming home late and I would want to go out with my friends, I started making my own meals or my mother would cook meals at different times for us. At night, after he'd had his dinner he would start drinking and he'd be up and down, topping up his glass.

Sometimes we would watch the news together: from time to time there would be a report of a child who had been abducted or murdered or raped, and he would sit there and say, 'These people should be hanged.' I would sit there and look at him and think to myself, 'That's you they're describing.' But he couldn't see that he was just like them: he wasn't like that – those people were sick and should be hanged – he wasn't sick; he wasn't like them.

I was beginning to realise more and more that what he was doing to me was wrong. I still wasn't aware of the word 'abuse'. I just knew this wasn't happening to everybody and wasn't normal, but I felt powerless to stop it. In fact, the more I realised his behaviour had to be abnormal, the more unhappy he made me. I started to feel he didn't love me at all. Because the attention he was showing me was perverted, he actually must have disliked me intensely to abuse me in this way. The innocence of my earlier thinking was giving way to a dreadful dawning that what was happening to me was dark and dangerous. Would it ever end? I became increasingly preoccupied with thoughts of what I could do to stop him.

I used to fantasise about taking a knife to bed with me and stabbing him, but I was too frightened to do it. I also used to fantasise about hurting him in some way. I don't know if I actually wanted to kill him; I just wanted the abuse to stop. I would fantasise about hurting him in some way so that he would get off me. In my head I had a clear scenario that after I'd hurt him I would have a small bag with some clothes in so that I could run away. I would run: I didn't know whom I would run to, but I would run and tell someone. I wouldn't tell my mother, but I would tell someone. I would run out of the back door of the house, across the large lawn, past the rhododendron bushes, down a walkway which led to the River Annan, and from there I could walk to Brydekirk. I knew that pathway really well, and because I believed I could outrun him, I would be able to get away. I went through this escape plan in my head umpteen times, but it never happened.

During this time my brothers still visited us at weekends occasionally, but Dianne was married so we saw less of her now. I missed seeing her. Although she was so much older than me, we had become fond of each other and an understanding had grown between us.

Life at the local school was becoming a farce. I wasn't happy there. I did less and less work, and so my grades were poor. This annoyed my father because in his eyes we were the people in the big house and should do nothing to blacken the Forester-Smith name. 'There is no one else called Forester-Smith,' he would tell me. 'If you do something wrong it will always be with you.' I think the headmistress turned a blind eye towards me because she rarely challenged me about my work, or lack of it. I think in her eyes I was the girl from the big house, and as she rented one of our bungalows I suppose my father was her landlord!

But when I went to Annan Academy in August 1980, I started to work again. I remember particularly enjoying my German class. I was ecstatic when I came twenty-first out of 300 in the year taking the German exam. I was absolutely delighted! I told my father, but to my disappointment he said, 'Well, why aren't you first?'

I said, 'But I'm twenty-first out of 300.'

But he said again, 'But why aren't you first?'

I was really discouraged then and decided just to give up again. There seemed to be no way of pleasing him. I remember that decision to this day. He was so determined that my education was to be the making of me. And it wasn't just my education. He told me to watch how I dressed, to watch what I said and whom I spoke to, and to be careful whom I mixed with. I started to rebel against every single thing he advised me to do. I threw away my whole education, which gave me great pleasure because he was paying for it.

I didn't particularly choose my friends at school, but I ended up becoming friendly with three girls in particular. We would walk to the town in our lunch breaks. At first we bought single cigarettes – that was possible in those days!

There was an arcade in Annan with rows of fruit machines and space invader games, and we used to spend a lot of time and money there. We weren't supposed to be there, because we were only thirteen and legally you had to be sixteen to play on the machines. Gradually we started to go there during our break times as well. We'd smoke our cigarettes, sometimes behind the school in an area we called 'smokers' corner', and we got away with it for a while.

At home the abuse continued as usual. He would regularly come into my bedroom, wake me up, masturbate himself, and the next morning, as usual, nothing was said. He would often give me a £5 note the morning after an incident had happened.

He never said to me, 'This is for you to keep quiet'; rather, 'Here's a wee extra for you.' But I knew what it was for.

When we moved to Luce he bought me two horses, Dusty and Match. I'd loved Dusty for years and had often ridden him at the riding school owned by my Aunt Elspeth – he was my favourite. But gradually I was growing out of him. I was growing taller and he was only about 11 or 12 hands. However, my dad bought him for me, and again I saw it as another bribe. He'd then buy me a new saddle or a new pair of riding boots. I now understand that this is typical behaviour; people who are victims do get bought things. For some it's lollipops. But because my dad was wealthy, I was given more extravagant presents.

I was becoming more and more rebellious. At home I would argue with my parents and answer them back. Outside the house I was considered daring, fun and wild. When we had lived in West Calder my mum often used to organise a disco for the Guides and Brownies. These had been great fun, and so I persuaded her to do a similar thing in Brydekirk because it was so dead; there was nothing for children to do together in the evenings. I preferred to mix with people four or five years older than myself, especially boys. There was one boy in particular that I was very fond of. I just loved him. In fact everyone loved him. He was good-looking and every girl in the village wanted to be his girlfriend. And he was really, really nice. I led him on and on and on, and I wanted him to have sex with me, not because I found it pleasurable but because I believed that if he had sex with me it would mean he really liked me, he really loved me. If he didn't, there was something wrong. However, all we ever did was kiss! He was a complete gentleman. (He is a Christian now.)

When my mum organised these discos, I would steal a bottle of drink from my dad's drinks cabinet, maybe a bottle of Martini or Cinzano. I would sit, with my friends, in the back room of the village hall without my mother knowing, and we'd drink and smoke. I don't know what my friends thought about me, because I certainly wouldn't have wanted to mix with people four or five years younger than me. But I suppose, in a way, I was a lot more mature than my peers. I had had to grow up with all that was being done to me by my father; I was certainly more sexually aware than most of my peers.

I was changing quickly now and becoming more and more rebellious. I started to go to Lockerbie ice rink at the weekends. I was allowed to do that because we were accompanied by a responsible adult, a girl who took her younger sister. When I was there, my clothes started to get more and more outrageous. I would leave the house wearing leggings and a baggy t-shirt. When I got to the ice rink, these would come off and I'd put on my bleached jeans and umpteen earrings, and spike my hair up; I was going through a punk phase. My parents knew. They were worried and I dare say they wondered where it was all going to lead. But I was having fun because I knew it was worrying them and winding them up. Then, because I was allowed to go skating, I got into the habit of not going skating!

I remember one occasion when I arranged to meet a friend in Brydekirk for the evening, a girl whose horse used to share a field with my horses. Although she was two or three years older than me, we had become good friends. On this particular occasion I told my parents I was going skating, but just after I left the house I hid my skates under a bush. On the way home I went to retrieve my skates, only to find they weren't there! I thought somebody had stolen them. But to my horror, when I arrived home they were sitting on the doorstep – my father had found them! To this day I still don't know how he found out. Needless to say, we had a huge argument and my dad called me a tart and a liar, and refused to let me go out again. It was strange, really, because when he behaved like that, showing concern for his daughter, he was just behaving like a normal father. But he hated the thought of me hanging around with older men, mixing with the local young people who hung around the village bus stop, the swing park or on the steps of the pub. He hated this because he would say I was sitting with peasants. But in Brydekirk there was nothing else to do!

He would have preferred me to stay at home. He didn't like the local people; they didn't speak well; they didn't dress well; they weren't educated; they weren't from anywhere, and as far as he was concerned, they weren't going anywhere.

I sometimes wonder if he regretted moving us to Brydekirk. The only consolation was the big house. But I was becoming a problem to him, especially at school.

After I was caught smoking, the headmistress summoned my parents to tell them about my unacceptable behaviour and how I was mixing with 'the wrong people'. She was obviously in awe of my father because he was well known in the local community, with a considerable amount of influence. She took the position of being very concerned for me, 'his poor daughter', rather than threatening to expel me. But finally my father lost patience and took me away from that school altogether. He reached the decision that if I was mixing with the wrong people it was better to send me somewhere else.

5

Can anybody help?

So in January 1982 I was sent to Rickerby Preparatory School in Ecclefechan. I was just fourteen years old. Originally for boys only, this school had just started admitting girls. When I joined there were seventy-five boys and five girls in the school!

On one hand, with the abuse at home continuing unabated, I found it hard being the only girl in the class; the other girls in the school were much younger, so I had nobody to confide in and be friendly with. I felt lonely here at first.

On the other hand, I was confident about my sexuality and enjoyed flirting with the boys both in and out of school. I had one particular boyfriend at this time, but nothing sexual happened between us. Eventually, the novelty of being the only girl in the class wore off and everyone got used to me being there. I was looked upon as being one of the lads to a certain extent, but I wasn't allowed into their gangs because at the end of the day I was a girl, and I wasn't even a boarder; I went home every night.

The school matron was quite young and very friendly, but I was very unhappy there and the initial feelings of loneliness increased. Also, around this time, I had told one of my friends in Brydekirk that my dad came into my room at night and was having sex with me. She told another girl who already disliked me because I had been friendly with her brother! And before I knew it, this story had spread round the village. As gossip does, the story had become embellished, and by the time I heard it, it was being said that I was encouraging my dad to have sex with me. So once again I had to learn the hard way that nobody would believe my version of events and it was better to keep quiet than speak out and risk being at best misunderstood, at worst maligned.

I felt so trapped and unhappy that one day I decided to run away. I had gone to school as usual, and after the morning lessons and lunch, I knew we had a sports lesson in the afternoon. I changed into my games kit, which to me looked like fairly normal clothing, and made my escape. I hitched a lift from the A74 at Eaglesfield to Melrose, in the Borders. That was where my gran lived, with my Aunt Elspeth.

My gran was pleased to see me. At first she thought someone had brought me, and was keen for me to bring them into the house! When I told her I had run away from school and come on my own, she was really surprised and wanted to know why I didn't want to go back home. She asked me a lot of questions, searching for information. I made up a story that I didn't like school and my father was being too strict with me. I begged my gran to let me stay with her and longed to talk to her and tell her the truth about what was happening to me. She was the one person I knew I could trust, and I knew she loved me.

But I couldn't come out with it. Whether or not it was the guilt I felt at running away from school and the inevitable recriminations that would result, the pressure of the moment stopped me from sharing my little secret with her. She was wonderful and very understanding, but eventually she rang my mother, and my parents came over the next day to collect me and take me home.

Of course, they then wanted to know why I'd run away. So once again I had to make up a story about how the boys had been picking on me and I didn't want to stay at that school any longer.

It was at that point in my life that I really wanted somebody to ask me a direct question. I felt that if I was asked the right question I could tell them about the abuse. But somehow it never happened. I lived in hope. I longed for the abuse to stop. That's all I wanted. I was terrified of my father. I wanted to protect my mother. I was very afraid of what might happen and what the consequences might be of him being found out. I wanted somebody to stop it and for everything to change but I couldn't bring myself to say anything – it's as though I was paralysed with fear. Maybe if somebody had pushed me enough I would have said something. Or if somebody had asked me straight out, was my father abusing me, that would have given me the opportunity I was looking for. But with my limited experience of sharing or hinting at the problem being so unsuccessful, I really had no confidence that anybody would believe me. After all, my father was so well known in the district, and well liked, it would have been his word against mine. I was so afraid of him. He was a big strong person and I couldn't see him leaving home or me being allowed to go and live with my grandparents. So I had no option, as I thought, but to go home and just put up with it.

If I had known then that my father had abused my sister Dianne as well, things may have been very different. But it was to be another couple of years before I discovered these things. At this time I thought I was the only one who had been abused, and so for the first fourteen years of my life I carried this secret alone.

After this my time at Rickerby came to an abrupt end, and in August 1982 I was sent to Wellington Girls' School in Ayr where I was a weekly boarder. I didn't really want to go away to this school, even though it meant that I would be safe from abuse for a few nights every week.

It's a curious thing, but somehow the familiar, as horrendous and frightening as it was, was comforting; it was awful but I knew what to expect. I knew when the emotional and physical agony of the abuse would start and I knew when it would finish. I hated every minute of it. But I suppose, over the years, I had learnt to cope by blocking out my feelings and being impassive; at least that way it was all over faster. At this stage I hadn't really had the courage to resist my father's abnormal behaviour towards me. Running away seemed my only escape route at this time; and I hadn't been very successful there. The thought of going to live in a school where I didn't know anybody meant making myself vulnerable yet again. And it all seemed so unfair; after all, I was not the perpetrator of this crime. If anybody should be leaving home, I thought, it should be my father. I felt that even though I was the innocent party, I was having to pay for his crime; he was able to stay at home while I was sent away.

I feel I can understand what children go through when they are sent to foster parents to escape violence at home. They are not the ones who should be re-housed; the guilty party should be taken out of the home so that the rest of the family can get on with their lives and live in peace and security, free from the fear of the person who is causing their pain.

But I consoled myself with the fact that if I was away from home I was, at least, spared some nights of abuse. However, I had to go home every weekend. Most of the time I would go by bus and my father would meet me at Dumfries and take me the short distance home. I hated these journeys. When he was in the car with me he would often put his hand on my knee and slide his hand up my leg. I would push it away. Every night that I was home I could guarantee everything would happen just like before.

So, in an attempt to avoid going home, I told my parents I wanted to be a fortnightly boarder, and the excuse I gave was that I was getting friendly with some of the girls. That worked, so then I pushed to be away for three weeks at a time. I knew my mother missed me so I would pluck up courage and go home for the odd weekend. Sometimes my father would come and collect me from school. How I dreaded these journeys. I would tell him I was tired and lie down in the back of the car. But on at least a couple of occasions I remember he stopped the car in a remote lay-by and climbed into the back of the car with me, and the abuse would start all over again. I wanted to jump out of the car and run away, but I was too scared because I didn't know where I was or where I could go to be safe.

Looking back on these times, it was a very risky thing for him to do. Anybody could have driven into those lay-bys and seen what he was doing; he was well known in the area and would have been easily recognised. But I think over the years he'd got away with so much and was therefore confident that he would not be found out. I later learnt that he used to take Dianne away to hotels on business trips with his friends – I can't help but think some of his friends must have wondered what was going on.

So on the Friday evenings that I went home the battle began. Just occasionally one of my brothers would meet me in Dumfries to take me home. He would let me drive even though I was only sixteen and hadn't passed my driving test! But usually it was my dad who came, and if I sat in the front of the car he would put his hand on my leg and tell me how much he'd missed me. I knew what he meant. I knew that later that night he'd come into my bedroom. I was getting really sick of it and kept wondering how I could stop it happening; but the only way I could see was by not being there.

On the one hand I was now a teenager with my own mind and strong opinions; but when I walked through my parents' front door I started to behave like an eleven- or twelve-year-

43

old again. The power that he exerted would cause me to regress so that whatever he said, I did. Then I would think about this and the anger would bubble up inside me and I would become argumentative and rebellious. But always he was the stronger, and I would be left feeling the helpless victim.

At school there were three matrons in the boarding house. I wondered if I should talk to one of them. Or maybe I could trust one of my new school friends. But then I reasoned with myself that if I told my friends what was happening to me at home, the matrons would hear about it and would feel duty bound to contact my parents; so there seemed no way out.

When the Easter holidays arrived I had to go home, and I really didn't want to. There were a few girls staying at school over the holiday because their parents lived in the Arab Emirates and it was considered too far for them to travel there and back. I wanted to stay at school with them. So on this particular Friday morning I was so upset about having to go home that I took a handful of paracetamol tablets and washed them down with a bottle of blue fountain-pen ink.

My English teacher was the first to find me and took me to the sick bay. I'd only taken six or seven tablets but I was sent to the local hospital to be checked by a doctor. The school was now very aware that something was wrong with me. My English teacher, whom I liked and respected, asked me what was upsetting me. I told her I just didn't want to go home.

'Why don't you want to go home?'

'I just don't want to go home. I want to stay here. I don't get on with my parents.'

'Is there something going on with your dad?' she asked me, insinuating that maybe he was physically violent towards me. She was trying to encourage me to talk. But I couldn't tell her.

But when she told me that my father was on his way to pick me up I really freaked.

'I can't help you unless you tell me what's wrong,' she pleaded.

So I missed another opportunity, perhaps the best opportunity I had created, to tell somebody about the abuse I was experiencing at home.

I think that if she had asked me more directly to tell her what was going on at home I could have begun to say. But just to ask me 'what's wrong?' was too vague. I realised this some years later when the police questioned me about my father. When they asked me directly whether I was being abused, I was able to say yes, and that made the whole process much easier. It may have been because I was older; but I prefer to think that it was the way the question was framed that encouraged me to have the confidence to talk and tell them the whole sordid story. If only I could have spoken up earlier.

When I got home my mum was very concerned and kept asking the same questions as my English teacher.

'Are you OK? Why did you do it?'

I just replied that I didn't like school and was really upset because I wasn't getting on with the girls. It seemed a valid excuse and stopped her asking questions.

But when my father came into my bedroom the following night I could take no more and started screaming. Hearing this my mum came running into my bedroom, and switching on the light saw my father next to my bed.

'What is going on?' she shouted.

'He's trying to get into bed to have sex with me.'

'What do you mean?'

'He's always doing this,' I screamed back at her.

'Right,' she said, 'downstairs.'

So the three of us went downstairs into the living room. My mother asked me if it was true. My father went out of the room, then returned; he kept walking in and out, accusing me of being mad and making up stories. He said I needed to see a shrink. I told my mother that it was true, and she said we needed to call the police and that we would leave the house that night and never come back if that's what I wanted. She asked if I was sure it was him and not my brother. I told her it was definitely my father – I could tell the difference between my brother and my father, and in any case he'd been doing this for years.

She was upset by now and left the room for about a minute, returning in a state of extreme anxiety.

'Is this true?' she asked. 'Are you sure you want to go ahead and call the police?'

I suddenly got scared. The situation was getting out of hand. I didn't want to leave my home. I wanted it to stop or him to leave. I panicked. I just couldn't cope with it. It wasn't that she was being aggressive. But she left the choice to me. I was fourteen years old. I was too young to make that decision.

So I said I was lying and nothing more was said.

6

Nobody knows you're here

So my attempts to stop the abuse had failed yet again. My despair of ever escaping from this circle of terror and misery deepened. I was fourteen years old, crying on the inside, confident on the outside. I was a prisoner, yet innocent of the crime for which I was paying such a high price.

Perhaps if I had realised then that my sister Dianne had also been abused by our father, I would have been more courageous and spoken out sooner. Perhaps we would have acted together and sought help and been rescued sooner.

The night I screamed and my mother came running into my bedroom, I was the only child in the house; my brothers and Dianne were all away. In fact, all through our childhood he had kept all of us children, and other close members of the family, apart. We rarely lived in the same house at the same time. We were even sent to different schools. I think now that it was quite deliberate.

So I returned to Wellington Academy for a further year. By this time I was sixteen years old. My parents wanted me to stay on for another year at least but I refused. I wanted to leave

47

school. I wanted to leave home. I had no ambition, only to leave home and never return.

I thought about becoming a rock star, or an actress. I'd always enjoyed dancing and drama, but I'd never pushed myself at school. I also enjoyed working with horses. I even enjoyed going to race meetings and wanted to drive racing cars like my father! He was an amateur driver and used to drive with Jackie Stewart and Graham Hill. He knew Murray Walker and James Hunt. He'd taken portrait photographs of all these men; they were hung at the top of the hall in our house. I could never look at them. To me it seemed as if their eyes were my dad's eyes. When I walked past them I felt as though he was watching me.

So I left school and went to live back at home. I had nowhere else to go. The strange thing is, I really didn't want to leave my home. I started going to college and was drawn to a group who enjoyed smoking and drinking, and inevitably, perhaps, I started experimenting with drugs.

For the first time in my life I was tasting freedom. At college I could be who I wanted to be, not just a little girl. I was meeting people with their own minds, people who accepted me for who I was. I was happy just to fit in with them and go along with the crowd rather than being controlled by my parents. It felt fantastic but also sad, because I quickly realised what a rubbish childhood I'd had and how bizarre my parents were. But I tried not to dwell on that too much. I obviously had a lot of anger bottled up inside and it came out with me being really really loud and outrageous just to get people's attention.

I also enjoyed upsetting people I didn't like – like some of my teachers. I started going out on drinking binges. Most people would have one gin, but I would have four! I soon had the reputation of being good fun, the mad one, the party goer, the centre of attention.

I started hanging out at a pub called the Joker. It was a

notorious place for buying drugs; in fact, if you walked into the place you didn't have to buy any drugs, you could just as easily get high on the fumes!

I started to go out with one of the barmen there. I didn't find him that attractive. It's hard to say whether I really liked him or not; but I went out with him just to annoy my parents. I was always taking something – hash, popping pills, I'd taken magic mushrooms by then, too. I made excuses to stay away from home by saying I was going out with my mates. Here, I thought, I was mixing with people who really had their heads screwed on; they talked about the environment and philosophy. It was exciting and I ended up sleeping with them all.

I didn't enjoy sex until I was nineteen. Until then it was just something I had to do to get a guy. When I was seventeen I wanted to get it over and done with just to make him happy. So I thought I was having a good time; everything seemed to be going reasonably well, until I discovered I was pregnant.

I was going out with a lad who wasn't at college and he already had another long-term girlfriend. I just flirted so much around him that he definitely knew I was interested and we began meeting together in secret. He was twenty at the time, three years older than me, which made him quite a lot wiser in my eyes. I suppose I was quite immature in some ways. He had his own car and motorbike; short hair and tattoos; he was a punk and into fighting – the sort of boy I just knew my parents would hate!

I loved punk music; it was aggressive and that is how I felt, so it matched my mood perfectly. I thought he was wonderful. We had a relationship which lasted between four and five months, after which time I realised I was pregnant. When I told him he asked me, 'How do you know it's mine?'

I knew I'd had several boyfriends, but I only ever saw one at a time so I knew this was his baby. But that was it, I went off and had an abortion. I went by myself to see a doctor. I didn't tell my boyfriend. I told my mother. I felt I had no choice as

I would be away for a night and couldn't think of a good enough excuse as to why I needed to be away, and I didn't want the college phoning her to find out why I wasn't there. She was very upset and asked me who the father was. I told her I didn't know; I didn't want her knowing. She asked me if I wanted to keep the baby, but I said no, I wanted an abortion, and I had it all arranged for the following day.

She was quite good about it. Dad never found out, even though my mum drove me to the hospital and picked me up the following day. She tried to encourage me to keep the baby and promised that we could find a way of managing. I could tell she understood and wanted to give me the option of keeping the baby – an option she once didn't have, I now believe.

I didn't think of the baby as a human being. I was just pregnant and wanted an abortion. It was six months later that I really thought about it. I didn't see the baby's father for two months; I wanted nothing more to do with him. But then he started to get interested in me again and that's when I discovered that I could use sex as a means of getting back at men.

I agreed to meet him one night. He picked me up in his van, which was a two-seater 'passion wagon'. We climbed into the back and I made sure he really enjoyed himself and felt fulfilled. He obviously did, because he wanted to see me again. But I didn't want to see him again, so I told him, 'Sorry, that's it.'

The sex he enjoyed with me was so good he wanted more; even ten years later he still wanted me! I had learnt how to use sex to control men. I felt powerful for once, and that's when I started to enjoy my sexuality and use it to my own advantage for a change.

In August 1985, just after the abortion, I decided to leave home. My granddad was ill and my Aunt Elspeth needed help with running the riding school. I agreed to help her for six weeks and ended up staying for six months. I would have stayed longer, but Elspeth and I fell out over my drug-taking. In the mornings, when I needed to be up and helping her with the horses, I was often hung over. My lifestyle got too much. I was helping at the riding school during the day and working in a club at night. It was the last straw for Elspeth when I painted my bedroom yellow. She was already tired of me changing my hair colour regularly; one day it was ginger, the next green!

I loved the horses. My aunt was very patient with me and let me keep my horse Pepper in her stables, and she bought Dusty from me while I was working for her. She even fed me as well! My dad would send me some money occasionally, and with my work at the night club I managed to pay for the drugs I was taking; I was spending all my money on drugs. I suppose my emotions were really frozen. I blocked out the pain by taking drugs. I didn't think about the past. I lived one day at a time. I had no ambition. My mind shut down. My body shut down. I don't remember any birthday parties because I don't think I ever had one. But after the disagreement with Elspeth I had no option but to move back home. I can understand now why she must have got fed up with me. She had a business to run, and my behaviour was becoming increasingly unpredictable.

I had an affair, which lasted on and off for seven years, with a man called Steve who had worked for my dad since he started his business in the garage at the back of the house. By now the business had grown and Dad owned an industrial estate called Marquis of Scotland, where he employed thirty people. He rented out the other buildings on the industrial estate to other businesses and consequently was very well known and highly thought of by the local business community. Steve enjoyed working for my father; he liked him and was proud to be part of the Forester-Smith 'empire'.

It was when I was sixteen that Steve and I started talking to one another. We would go skating together. I quite liked him.

He was a decent lad and treated me with respect, being younger and the boss's daughter! When I returned home, however, we started having a relationship. He treated me well. He was very quiet. We went to the cinema on Saturday nights. He was quite shy; it took him about a month before he would hold my hand in public. He was so nice; he didn't just want sex, but it slowly developed into a sexual relationship. But after a couple of months I was desperate to leave home again, so in 1986 I sold Pepper (he went to a good home) and I left and went to live in Melrose. I stayed there for a year, but it was hard for me to settle and put roots down. My father would frequently send one of my brothers over with letters saying he would cut me out of his will unless I returned to live at home. These letters filled me with dread. I found them threatening and I would feel physically sick with anxiety. Even when I was away from home, he was able to control me; I felt like a child again. So eventually I capitulated and returned home to work for my dad.

By this time I was taking a lot of drugs, including acid. I really enjoyed it. It didn't freak me out; I didn't see big white rabbits or try to fly, but I did have the giggles and would laugh about anything. Time stood still; hours would seem like minutes. But coming down would be awful. Elspeth would tell me my mood swings were quite bad and I would get very depressed and irritable. I hated men, but loved drugs. I'd do anything for drugs. Some mornings I would wake up and not know where I was. One minute I was working behind a bar, the next morning I would wake up to find a pair of feet next to me and I'd not know whom they belonged to.

I remember meeting one chap, he was from Pakistan. He felt he could do what he liked to women over here because in his culture all white women were trash. The weekend I met him I felt really attracted to him. He had dark eyes, and plenty of drugs, amphetamines. We must have spent the weekend taking these tablets, because when I weighed myself on the

Monday I'd lost a stone and a half. A lot of it must have been fluid, but I just didn't want to eat and because I didn't want to eat I ended up taking more and more tablets.

On this particular weekend we were staying in a flat in Galashiels which belonged to a friend. I can't remember why, but we decided to go back to the riding school to collect some belongings I had left there. When we arrived, my granny was at home and came out to meet us. She was pleased to see me, but she took one look at this chap and I could tell from the expression on her face, not to mention her body language, that she didn't like him at all. Sadly we had a huge argument because I pleaded with my gran to let us stay with her but she refused. I asked her to explain her reasons; after all, she'd let my other boyfriends stay in the house. But Gran had taken an instant dislike to this guy and she was not going to change her mind. The more I pleaded with her, the more she resisted. That was the only argument I've ever had with my gran. She was obviously really upset to see me with this man. But what could I do? I could hardly tell him to go away! So, in the end, realising that my chances of getting Gran to change her mind were nil, and feeling very angry towards her, I said that if she wouldn't let him stay then I wouldn't stay either. And with that, we got back into the car and drove away.

The next weekend I went out with him again, and instead of taking me to Galashiels he took me to Edinburgh. Now he had a drug habit as well, and on this particular day he was taking hash and driving at the same time, which was pretty scary. But I used to smoke with him, and smoke so much that it would all seem a bit of a laugh and we forgot the danger we were putting ourselves in. I knew I didn't feel right and shouldn't be with him. So we were getting ourselves stoned and driving to Edinburgh and I realised I didn't know where I was. I knew Edinburgh, having lived there in the past. But on this occasion I didn't recognise where he was taking me. We stopped the car outside a building. He took me to his flat and locked the door. As I was sitting in the living room he turned round to me and said, 'Who knows you're here?'

'Nobody.'

'That's good.'

'What do you mean?'

'Anything could happen to you, you're here with me and nobody knows I live here.'

I just freaked. 'What's going on? Are you trying to frighten me?'

He was being very weird and bizarre. He took me upstairs. I went along with him. I knew there was a good party in Galashiels that night so I used all my powers of persuasion and managed to convince him to drive me back there.

I had been really scared, and as we drove back I realised how much danger I'd been in. We did get back and I didn't see him again. He went on to the next person, but it was events like that which made me think and I started to take more care of myself. I didn't stop drinking or taking drugs, but I stopped drinking so much and didn't smoke so much either. I did more acid, which I suppose some people would think is more scary, but to me it was better because I felt aware and in control of my mind.

I scared myself sometimes. I could have been murdered. I was asking for trouble. I believe now that God had his hand on me because I don't know how I survived that time.

7

The secret gets out

I'd been scared. But that experience was soon forgotten and my life continued as before – working at the night club, taking drugs, sleeping around. My father wanted me to go back home and live there. He kept phoning me and sending me letters. He'd tell me my mother was upset that I wasn't around and I was breaking her heart. So I'd go home occasionally to see my mum and she'd ask if I was happy. I'd say, 'Yes, I'm happy and I'm staying over there, life's great, I've got a job.'

Then my dad would start trying to bribe me to go back home to live. 'If you come home you can have anything you want, you can have more horses, you can do this, you can do that.'

But I didn't want to go home!

I met a guy called Martin and moved in with him and we started living together. This really upset my dad. I think it was not because I was living in sin; rather, he was jealous that another man was having me. Martin was nice enough but I knew our relationship was never going to last. For a time I enjoyed the security he offered. I was working longer and longer hours at the night club and still taking a variety of drugs.

It wasn't long before I was unfaithful to Martin. With my work, I was constantly meeting other men, and sleeping with them was an inevitability for me at that time. This happened because Martin's work took him away from time to time; he was studying part time and had to attend lectures. So if he went away for a weekend, I would go out partying.

Then I fell pregnant again. This time I could not be sure who the father was. So although I wasn't upset at being pregnant, I could not be sure Martin was the father, and I didn't want him to know I'd been sleeping around while he'd been away. Therefore, in my own mind I decided to get rid of the baby. I told him I was pregnant. It was really odd. He was very happy and he wanted the kid and that terrified me. I just wanted him to say I should have an abortion. I didn't want the kid because having a child meant that I would have to commit myself to Martin and I wasn't totally in love with him. And to me, at that time, every man was a potential abuser and I didn't want the father of my child involved in the child's life just in case what had happened to me happened to them.

I was nineteen years old. I just couldn't handle this, it was all getting too serious.

Martin had to go away for one of his study weekends so I actually arranged to have an abortion while he was away. I went up to Edinburgh and booked myself into a clinic. I told my friend who lived in Edinburgh. She invited me to stay with her the night before. She was very kind and took me to the clinic the next morning and collected me later that day and took me back to her place. When I saw Martin again, I told him I'd had a miscarriage, and to this day he thinks that's what really happened. On hearing the news he was quite emotional and he asked me to marry him. I said yes. But the next day I picked an argument with him and left.

I was quite deliberately calculating. I had to get out of this relationship quickly. That's what I used to do to everybody who got too close to me. I didn't want anybody getting that close. I'd been hurt by the one man I should have been able to trust most in my life and I was not going to allow anybody to hurt me again; that was my thinking then. So I deliberately started an argument to create a opportunity that gave me an escape route.

And for a while I went back to live at home. I had nowhere else to go. I was depressed, really unhappy. During this time I would frequently descend into deep lows that lasted for many weeks. One minute I would be the life and soul of the party and everyone would see me; then all of a sudden I wouldn't go out for three or four weeks in a row because I didn't want to see anybody or contact anybody. I would just want to be on my own; really down; really depressed. Then I would snap out of it, take some drugs and go out and party. I suppose I never really dealt with anything. I just coped and lived from day to day.

It was suggested that I go to Germany to be an au pair. I thought it seemed like a good idea. I had enjoyed speaking German at school and it meant I could get away from home and Martin. My dad liked the idea because it took me away from Martin; and despite all that had happened between us, there was still a part of me that liked him. So it was hurriedly arranged, and I went off to Germany for a couple of months on a short-term contract. The family were very kind but I couldn't handle being on my own for long hours with no company of my own age, and before long I decided to return home.

So I came back and started working for my dad – again. It seemed to me at the time to be an easy option. In any case, I didn't know what else I could do. I couldn't go and live with any of my other relatives and I needed a job. My dad offered me a job and a home. I was living in his house free of charge and the abuse had stopped, so I thought this was an easy ride.

I was confident enough to believe that the abuse had stopped for good by this time, and I felt as though the events of the past three or four years had helped me to discover myself. For once, I felt I was my own person, so there was no way I would allow him to start abusing me again. I suppose I felt more in control of my own life and therefore of what he could do to me. Maybe he sensed that I was no longer the helpless child that he could coerce. I was no longer afraid of him in the way I used to be, and I think he realised just how much I'd changed and how assertive I'd become. He was happy to have me at home and was generous with his money. I think, if anything, he thought he could control me now by threatening to cut me out of his will if I didn't please him. In his view, money was a powerful weapon and an effective bribe.

When I look back on this time of my life it saddens me that I had no personal ambition or career. I left school early partly because I was afraid of failing. It was as though I always wanted to do something with my life but I was afraid to try in case I failed. I wanted to succeed at something. I wanted to be somebody in my own right and be known for being good at something. But I never believed it was possible. So I didn't try. I felt like that for a long time. Maybe it was something to do with my dad accusing me of not coming first in that German exam. I thought after that, well, if you can't come first, why bother to try? This attitude seemed to cloud my whole life then.

So I helped him with his recovery truck business. When I first started, I worked in the store room organising the stock control and the budgeting. I quite enjoyed the work. And, of course, I saw Steve again, which was fine. He was really nice; we got on well and enjoyed each other's company, the family liked him and so life was pretty easy.

I stopped taking drugs mainly because nobody in Annan took drugs, and apart from the odd drink everything was fine – quite dull in some respects! The family was reunited so we decided to go away together on a cruise. I was twenty-one and anorexic. I had finished with Steve – not for any particular reason, it just happened. But it was hard because he was still working for my dad and I was seeing him at work all the time. I didn't really want to finish with him although I was enjoying the freedom of being on my own again and spending some time with my girlfriends.

The cruise was a disaster. My father would insist I sat with them at mealtimes. I would refuse to eat anything. The arguments would get bigger and bigger and the scenes more dramatic. So I started eating and throwing it up, or I'd pretend to eat and cough the food into my napkin.

But at least my parents were in a cabin at the other end of the boat, so that was good. I used to organise parties in my cabin at night. If the ship was berthed we would go on shore and go sight-seeing during the day. After the evening meal, my mother would retire to her cabin and I would go to the disco and then, late at night, make my way to the bar, where I would find my dad. I would charge all my drinks to his account. I'd buy champagne for my 'friends' and spend a lot of money. I started getting friendly with the guys in the band. I'd buy them drinks and they'd buy me drinks. My dad would turn up and drag me away, calling me a tart and saying I was nothing but a whore. It was quite clear that he was jealous because he no longer had the control over me that he'd once enjoyed. He really embarrassed me until I realised that the people I was with thought his behaviour towards me was horrific. 'Is he like this all the time?' they'd ask. 'Is he drunk? How do you live in the same house as him?' I began to see there was a positive side to his behaviour; it was acting in my favour for once.

So each day on the cruise followed the same routine. Every morning we'd have an argument at the breakfast table and I'd refuse to eat. My mother would suggest we start each day afresh and try not to argue. I'd tell her about how Dad had been rude to me in the bar the night before, and embarrassed me in front of my friends.

So that was the cruise. I returned from what should have been the holiday of a lifetime feeling miserable. I'd lost a lot of weight. But then I met Graham. I don't know why, but as soon as I met him I started eating again. It took me a couple of years to really get back into a normal pattern of eating. But this was the start. I'd have one meal a day, or sometimes one meal every two days; but at least I was eating something and my family were pleased that Graham had started me eating again.

By now it was 1990 and I was twenty-two. Graham and I went out with each other for about eight months. The relationship was going well, but because I was having a relationship with someone else, Steve started being interested in me again. So I started seeing both of them and I made it perfectly clear to both of them what I was doing. Out of the pair of them I didn't know which one I preferred, but unfortunately I fell pregnant with Graham. I told Steve that I didn't want the baby. Graham didn't want the baby either so that was the catalyst for us finishing. I was secretly pleased he didn't want the child because that was the excuse I needed to have another abortion; it took the guilt away from me. Steve arranged for me to have the abortion carried out in a private clinic in Birmingham, and he even paid for it: that's the kind of amazing guy he was.

At this stage, I was living a wild life again. I visited the festivals, Glastonbury and Reading. I'd take acid and convince my friends to do the same. I was the life and soul of the party, but looking back I was reckless with my life. I was very nasty as well. Graham started going out with another girl. I had decided that he wasn't for me, that's why I was quite happy to end our relationship. But when I saw him going out with this other girl I made her life very difficult. They are married now and very happy together, which I'm really pleased about; but I was really awful to them then.

Strangely enough, we are all really good friends again now! I have changed, and they have changed. Over Christmas 2000, Cam and I met them and we had a wonderful evening together. I apologised to Graham's wife, and she apologised to me, which I thought was rather unusual and undeserved!

But to return to the events of 1990: on another occasion a chap I was going out with asked me if I could see myself having kids.

'Yes,' I replied, 'but only from a sperm bank.'

'Why?' he asked.

'Because I don't want the father of the kid involved.'

It was all to do with the abuse. I wanted to make sure that no man ever controlled my life again. I wanted no man in authority over me. I wasn't really enjoying life at this time; I was abusing other people. I was using sex as a control over men and in a way I was letting myself be abused again. Even though I thought I was in control, I wasn't.

So during the day I would work in the office, by this time organising the sales and admin, and then at night I'd work for a haulage contractor, driving HGVs up and down the country. Life continued like this for the next four years: drink, drugs and driving. My dad promised that one day I'd take over the business. Was that what I really wanted?

I had a few good friends, and because I was so fed up with living at home I suggested we move into a house together. They agreed so we looked around and found a house in Annan – there were four of us. I decided not to tell my parents until just before I was due to move. Everything was arranged in secret and we had a moving date.

We shared the house for about six months until one day one of the others decided to move out; they had found a job in another area.

I really didn't want to leave the house, but I couldn't afford to stay there, so once again I went home and resumed my relationship with Steve. By this time he had his own house so I lived with him most of the time. He was a very kind man, but once again I didn't feel I could trust him totally and I had affairs with other men even while I was living with him. I was also disappointed with him, because some months earlier we had been sat in a pub with some friends who were singing my dad's praises and saying what a kind and generous man he was. Afterwards I'd told Steve about how my father had abused me. He shouldn't have been surprised, because I first told him in 1987, after we'd been out drinking together. This time he was shocked but he didn't react negatively towards him, in the way that I'd have expected him to have done. I'd tell him how much I hated my dad, but he kept saying how nice he was, so I found that very odd. I felt he didn't want to believe me and that put a lot of distance between us.

Shortly before we broke up, I became pregnant again, with Steve's baby, but had an abortion without him knowing. Once again we drifted apart and I went back home to live. I was still working for my dad. Everything was normal and unexciting; I wasn't going out with anybody.

Life looked set to continue in this way.

But in February 1994 events took a bizarre twist when two female police officers arrived at the house and spoke to my mother. They were from the Woman and Child Protection Unit.

My mum phoned me at work. 'The police are here. Do you know what this is all about?'

'It will be about Dad.' I knew instinctively.

I drove back to the house and went in through the back door. Mum was standing there with our gardener/maintenance man, who was very friendly with her.

'What is this all about?' she asked again.

'It's all about your husband, my father, abusing me.'

'Just deny everything. Just say nothing happened,' she said.

I walked into the living room and sat down. One of the police officers told me that they'd had a telephone call to say that my father had been reported for abusing a young girl. Had he abused me as well?

'Yes,' I replied.

'Can you tell me about it?'

At last somebody had asked me the right question. It was such a relief for someone to ask me outright whether I'd been abused, and to be able to say a simple yes. And they believed me! It felt great. After all those years of wanting to be taken seriously, I could hardly believe it. At that point I didn't think about the wider picture or what might happen as a result of this meeting. It was so good to talk to somebody outside the family and to know that, at last, something was going to be done. In hindsight I think one of the reasons they acted so quickly was because my mum frequently held Guide and Brownie camps in the grounds of the house, and if my father was a child abuser then the implications were very serious. How many people had he abused?

We were told the court case would be held within six weeks, and within six months he'd be in prison. My overriding emotion was a sense of relief; I was just pleased that at last, after all these years and for the first time in my life, the awful truth had been revealed. No longer did I have to pretend. Our little secret was out.

8

The pendulum swings

It was my Aunt Elspeth who had heard that my dad had been abusing children and, needing to tell somebody, she told her husband, John. They had only recently been married, and clearly John had reacted strongly to these revelations and decided that the police should be informed immediately. My mother was extremely angry with her brother-in-law for telling the police. She told him he had only just married into the family and had no right to interfere with matters that were nothing to do with him. I, on the other hand, was delighted that he had taken the initiative.

But as these dark secrets were starting to emerge, the effect was to cause large ripples of fear and uncertainty throughout the family. One evening I sat down with Mum and told her my full, frightening story. As I described night after night of abuse, she just sat there smoking one cigarette after another. She became very agitated and then really upset and said she wanted to fling herself into the river. She really didn't know what to do. She felt as though her world was falling apart. The presence of police officers calling at our house only added to her anxiety.

Apparently John had made an anonymous phone call to the police to tell them he had heard on good authority that my dad was abusing kids and had easy access and contact with Guides and Brownies who frequently camped on his estate. So it was not surprising that the police moved fast, armed with this sort of information.

Once the police were involved, the rest of the family were told, much to my relief. At last, after all these years, I could say what I wanted, be who I wanted to be, and I didn't have to pretend that Dad was a good father. I felt liberated. At last I was no longer a silent victim; somebody had listened to me and believed my story. The right question had been asked, giving me the opportunity to speak up and reveal our little secret. I cannot adequately describe the utter relief I felt during these days. I felt vindicated, as though somebody had found the right key to unlock the door of my life that had been tightly shut and sealed all these years. Of course, I wondered what was going to happen next; I was well aware that I was surrounded by a very upset group of people. My mother didn't know what to do with herself. I daresay Elspeth felt that maybe her husband had acted unilaterally. But for me, the elation came from knowing that somebody had believed my story. I wasn't imagining it after all. It wasn't my fault this had happened to me. I had been abused, and now the perpetrator of that abuse would be brought to justice. At least, that is what I hoped. If I had known then that it would be many years before my father was finally brought to trial I might not have felt so relieved.

However, for those first few days of freedom, I was grateful. For that is how I felt: free. Free to no longer hide the horrible reality of my life. Free to no longer have to pretend. Free from secrets that had bound me all my life. Free to move out of the vicious circle that had encompassed me and become so familiar that now I felt on strangely new ground.

All this coincided with my friend Gem paying me a visit. She was living in Manchester at the time but came from Annan. She was a dancer for a band called Vertigo, and one of the singers in this band was a guy called Cam. It was Cam who drove her to my house that day and we all went out for a drink together.

Although Gem was a good friend, I didn't tell her about the events of the past few days because I didn't want to involve Cam. So we just sat and chatted. From the moment we met, I really liked Cam. There was something about him that was different to any of the other men I'd met. He was very loud and attractive. At that time I was dressing like a Goth. My hair was black, sometimes purple. I was wearing black make-up on my face and painted my fingernails black. I wore a lot of leather. The kind of guy I liked to be seen with then either had short black hair or really long black hair with make-up. Cam was different; he didn't look like that at all!

We sat and talked for about half an hour and then they were gone. That's what Gem was like!

Shortly after this I went down to Manchester to stay with Gem and her girlfriend, Trish. We all went to a night club called Cruze in the gay village in Manchester. Cam came too, and we had a great night out; I really enjoyed it. I felt a bit odd because I was into Grunge and Goth, Cure and Cult, that sort of music. Here it was all House music which I didn't really like; I found it repetitive and boring. Still, it was a night out.

The first thing Cam said to me was, 'Do you take drugs?' I said yes, so we went to the loo together.

This was a new experience for me, being in a toilet cubicle with a man; but in the gay village it happened all the time. Whatever loo was available you used, it didn't matter who you were, what you were or where you were! I had some acid and decided I was really enjoying myself with Cam although we were so different. He seemed a real showman. He liked being the centre of attention. He dominated the dance floor. I was used to doing that myself, but only when it was Goth music. I didn't like dancing to House music. So I was being quite quiet that night.

Also, I wasn't quite sure whether or not he was straight. After all, we were in a gay night club! And I could tell Cam was wondering the same thing about me. We danced as a group for a while. Another girl joined us and was flirting with Cam and Gem; she was bi-sexual. I just took it in my stride because I'd never been there before – this was a new experience for me and I was finding it exhilarating. I think it was the most hedonistic place I had ever been to; there seemed to be no taboos. People were enjoying themselves, enjoying being seen, and enjoying being free to be with whoever they wanted to be with. As the night drew on, although I was having a great time, there was one question I wanted an answer to – whether or not Cam was straight.

On the last song he asked me for a dance and I said, 'Oh, you're straight?'

'Yes.'

'So am I!'

And that was the start of our wonderful relationship. Something positive was going on in my life at the same time as the news about my father was breaking back home in Brydekirk.

Cam continued to intrigue me. He was far more flamboyant than any other man I'd met, and it wasn't just due to the drugs. Although at that time we were into completely different scenes, I really fancied him. He looked different from anyone else. He liked dressing up, which I do. He had recently been in a group called Bizarre Inc, which I thought sounded awful although they were very successful and popular at the time.

I actually think that's what attracted him to me at first; I wasn't impressed with his music but really liked him as a person. I had recognised him because one of my Goth friends had shown me a picture of his band, and as far as I was concerned, before I met him, he was the daft dancer with long hair! He didn't have long hair when I met him, which was just as well because it would have been the wrong type of long hair. It had to be straight and black and Cam's hair was curly! It was all very strange, and I believe it was God who brought us together because, in the natural, he was not my type of person. Wrong music, wrong crowd, wrong looks!

So I started to spend my weekends in Manchester with Cam, and worked for my dad during the week. I was doing a lot of driving! Now that Dad was under police investigation the atmosphere at home had changed again. He would come into the office and give me work to do. I'd do the work but not talk to him. By this time, Nicola knew what was going on. She worked in the office with me.

'What are you going to do?' she would ask. 'You can't stay here.'

I didn't know what to do. I was spending more and more time in Manchester with Cam. We would sit in Cam's flat and discuss what was going on. I'd told him about Dad soon after I'd met him. I had to. My moods were all over the place. Plus Gem and I talked; she knew about my past. So if Cam came into the room and we suddenly stopped talking he soon realised we were holding something back from him.

So one night in bed I asked Cam if he had any dark secrets. He told me that his ex-girlfriend had had a child and he wasn't too sure whether or not it was his. So then I told him mine, that I'd been sexually abused by my dad. He sat bolt upright in bed. Now this was meant to be a nice romantic evening. We were in bed surrounded by candlelight and music, and he suddenly got really angry. He didn't want to know the details of exactly what my father had done to me, but he wanted to know why I still talked to Dad, why I went home, why I still worked for him, why I did this and why I did that.

I told him the police were involved and he was glad about that. But he was so angry and upset. I was quite taken aback by this reaction; never before had any boyfriend of mine been so protective towards me and angry towards my father. And this news really made Cam take an instant dislike to him. He hated the thought of what he had done. He was mad that he'd got away with it for so long. He wanted to know how soon the police would have the evidence pieced together and the case could go to court; how long was my father to be free to roam wild, terrorising young children and women?

So on the one hand, Cam was impatient for my father to be brought to justice. But my mother was going through agonies at the same time. Her whole world had fallen apart. Everybody knew everything about her husband, and she would plead with me, 'Your dad's an old man, do you really want to see him in prison?'

She would say to me that if he went to prison she would just disappear because she couldn't live with the shame. She thought nobody would want to talk to her again, the work with the Guides and Brownies would have to stop, she'd have to move away so I'd lose both my parents. She tried her best to encourage me to drop the case.

One night she was crying, wishing that Dad would die.

'Do you mean that?' I asked.

'Yes,' she replied.

I suppose it was easy for me to cut myself off from my mother. After all, I'd spent the first three years of my life living with my grandmother and she was the one I really bonded with, she was the one person I trusted. Now my mother was beginning to feel a total stranger to me.

One day, I was alone in the office with my dad. I said to him, 'Can you not admit it to me? That's all I want, and this investigation could be dropped tomorrow. I just want you to say sorry and explain why you did this to me.'

'You're nuts,' was his reply.

'Look, there's only me and you here,' I pleaded.

'You're nuts.'

I walked out and left him in the office on his own.

The intensity of the situation was almost driving me crazy. I couldn't think straight. I resorted to taking more drugs; it was the only way I knew of blocking out the pain and the pressure. I can remember my mother was concerned that I might be heading for a nervous breakdown. Perhaps it was out of concern for me or perhaps it was her way of finding a way out of this mess and thus avoiding a court case, but she called me and asked me to go and see her. She wanted to talk. She had a plan.

We sat around a table and she gave me a blank sheet of paper. 'Write what you want from your father on this piece of paper in exchange for dropping the case completely.'

It seems ridiculous now, but I went upstairs and wrote this really stupid letter. I asked him to say sorry for all the hurt and abuse he'd caused. I decided I wanted £1,000 for every year that he'd wrecked my life. And I wanted two good holidays a year. I signed it, took it downstairs and handed it to my mother.

My mother read what I'd written. 'He won't sign anything with the word "abuse" in it,' she said. 'You'd better go away and write it again.'

I wrote the letter again, this time omitting the word 'abuse', and handed it to my mother.

My mind was in a whirl, the pressure was so intense. I needed to get right away for a while. So along with a friend called Pam and four lads that we used to go drinking with, I went to Gran Canaria on holiday. Cam didn't come. He was part of my Manchester life. These were my Scottish friends.

It was a brief respite, but in retrospect one that I was to regret taking because I returned home to find that the case against my father had been dropped completely. I couldn't believe it. Apparently, just after I'd left to go on holiday, a letter came from the Procurator Fiscal inviting me to go and discuss the case. I had already given my statement to the police. So, while I was away, Mum went to see the Procurator Fiscal and informed her I was dropping the case. The Fiscal was really angry, wanting to know why I was going to drop it. My mother apparently explained that I just couldn't handle the pressure and the responsibility of the consequences and didn't want to go ahead with it. The Fiscal was very disappointed because she knew we had a good case. But nevertheless it was dropped, and no further action was taken.

So that's how I got my holiday in Gran Canaria paid for, plus another holiday that year. I started receiving £100 a month, he paid for my overdraft and the case was dropped completely.

I felt let down by my mother because I knew that if she'd have said, 'Let's stand together on this, I will support you, I believe you,' then it would have been all right. As it was, the pressure on me was intolerable, but I was annoyed that my short holiday had allowed this to happen.

However, just as I thought I was free to pick up the tatters of my life, and carry on as though nothing untoward had happened, I was taken by a further surprise. Elspeth called to say she wanted to meet me. She said she had a story she wanted to share with me.

I could not have prepared myself for the shock that I was about to hear. She too had been abused by my father. After watching the events of the past few weeks, and doubtless feeling disappointed that the case had been dropped, she felt duty bound to tell me her story. She must have felt under extreme pressure, and being newly married, too. I cannot imagine how her husband John reacted when he heard that my father had abused her as well. I was staggered to hear this latest revelation.

For my mother, the news that her own sister was the next victim to step forward and tell the truth must have been a terrible blow. She was confident that, in persuading me to sign a sham letter agreeing not to take any further action, the case had been well and truly closed.

Once again the pendulum had unexpectedly swung, and

once again I was faced with an overwhelming dilemma – what would happen now?

9

The truth emerges

As Elspeth told us her story we were amazed. In 1971 she was engaged to a man from America. She met him when he came to work in the UK for a while. He was an actor. In order to break the news of their engagement tactfully to his family, he flew home to visit and speak with them in person. However, as he was undoubtedly anticipating, his family were not pleased with his choice of bride because he was a Catholic while Elspeth was a Protestant, and they strongly urged him to break off the engagement.

As far as Elspeth was concerned, the marriage was made in heaven and she was looking forward to being reunited with her fiancé in a few days' time. So it was a devastating shock when he phoned to tell her the engagement was broken.

She was distraught. 'The love of my life has broken our engagement because of my religion?' She couldn't understand it because, in her eyes, she wasn't a religious person; she wasn't even a practising Protestant; she hadn't been to church for years.

She went to see my mum, her sister, and sat crying as she

tried to come to terms with her loss. She talked and cried, trying to persuade herself that he would change his mind. As the evening wore on, the conversation changed little. My father gave her a drink. She later described to my sister and me how, although she only remembers my dad giving her one drink, she felt very sleepy very quickly, and finally Mum helped her into bed, putting her in the spare bedroom in the basement of the house.

When my mother eventually heard Elspeth's story, she told me how she and Dad then went up to their own bedroom and, as far as she was concerned, that was it; they both slept soundly until the next morning.

However, Elspeth told a different story because she described how, later that night, my father returned to her bedroom and she awoke to find him in bed with her. With total disregard to her objections, he raped her. Appalled, frightened and disgusted that he should take advantage of her especially when she had turned to them for comfort and support, and doubtless worried as to what her sister would think of her husband doing this to her, she hurriedly left the house leaving all her belongings behind, including her handbag, and drove to her mother's house nearby.

Elspeth hadn't mentioned this event to anybody until she told us, all those years later. Like me, she had kept this a secret, managing to disguise the memory and get on with her life as best she could. Apparently, according to Elspeth, my mother never questioned her as to why she had left our house in the middle of the night or why she had left her handbag behind.

My father, according to Elspeth, when challenged had retorted that, as far as he was concerned, she'd been flirting with him all evening and as good as 'invited' him to her bedroom.

So it was that in 1994, when she heard that the case had been dropped against my father, she came to tell us her story. I was really shocked; I could hardly believe what I had heard.

And I felt deeply sorry that this should have happened to Elspeth. I had always been very fond of her and she had been very good to me and often helped me out.

The Fiscal had told us, when we dropped the charges before, that if ever any new evidence came to light we could re-open the case. To be honest, at this point, on hearing these latest revelations from Elspeth, I wasn't sure whether we were ready to do this. We were under no illusions as to how difficult and emotionally draining it would be – and would it get us anywhere in the end? Having once dropped the case, I could not be certain that we would have the determination to stand together and see it through. And were we prepared for the public humiliation of having to relate our experiences in court and be made to re-live all those years of abuse and shame? I was almost at the point of drawing a line under the past and just getting on with my life as best I could, burying the past under the proverbial carpet.

I needed time to think. I felt so alone. I knew I'd been badly damaged emotionally by my father and that part of me was, as it were, entombed in ice, out of reach. Was I prepared to let the ice melt and discover that part of me that nobody, not even I, knew about? I often wondered what sort of a person I would have been if all this hadn't happened to me. I would watch other girls my age. They seemed so carefree in comparison to me. I knew I was a good actress and could put on a brave face; I was good at playing charades and being the life and soul of the party. I could be very loud and sociable. People would enjoy my company. But when I was on my own, I went into retreat. I so badly wanted to be different. I felt angry that what should have been the happiest years of my life had been stolen from me by a man who, I felt, had used me for his own selfish gratification.

So, after these new revelations, in November 1994 I left home for the last time and went to live with Cam. I took a job as a lorry driver working for an agency and life appeared to go back to normal, just as if nothing had happened.

Some of my extended family used to talk about my father when I saw them. They would start to cry and be sorry that they hadn't done more to help when I was younger. They would look back to the family gatherings we used to have, and with the benefit of hindsight tell me how they could now realise how unhappy I seemed. Now they chided themselves for not recognising the danger signs. I would sit and talk to them and tell them it wasn't their fault and try and offer them some modicum of comfort. How could they have guessed that things were as bad as they were, when not even I realised I wasn't the only one being abused at the same time? Such was the illusion of deception.

But Mum wouldn't talk about it at all and just carried on with her life as best she could; in fact, the pair of them just carried on with life as if nothing had happened. They even went away on holiday together – I just couldn't understand it. Actually it was really weird: a strange kind of truce, as if we were all in some kind of denial, not wanting to accept that if matters were taken further, to court, the family would be finally torn apart with no hope of repair. Or maybe it was because the truth was finally emerging, which simultaneously released some of the pressure that living with dark secrets had caused. It was certainly a relief for me to know that the abuse had stopped and my father had been found out.

We went back to visit them from time to time but Cam found it very difficult to cope with. So our visits became less and less frequent. Cam would say to me, 'Why do you want me to go back and listen to this guy talking about who he is and how well he's done and what a self-made guy he is when I know what he's done to my girlfriend?'

The final straw came during Christmas 1995 when my dad walked behind me and grabbed my bum. Cam saw him, and I saw that Cam had seen him. Cam was furious and we left Annan the next day and never went back.

By now Cam was working as a DJ in a night club in Blackpool and I worked behind the bar. I was also selling drugs to the other staff working in the club although Ian (another guy who worked there) and I were using more than we sold. Ian was a little suspicious of me when I first went to work there; he thought I only got the job because I was the DJ's girlfriend. However, I soon showed him I could do the job well and be popular with the customers at the same time, so we quickly became good friends. I loved him straight away; he was as camp as Christmas and great fun. The three of us used to go around together, often to other clubs where some of his friends worked. A few weeks later, we went skiing together in Andorra, and that's where Cam asked me to marry him and we became engaged!

On arriving home, reality hit us hard as we discovered the night club where we all worked had been closed for a few weeks. So Ian came to stay with us in our flat, and because we were all out of work we all signed on for our dole money. We thought we had our priorities right in making sure that we always had enough money to buy our drugs; fresh food came second. Our lives developed a certain routine; we went out a great deal at night to clubs where Cam could wangle free entry. And for a time we existed.

Eventually I found another job as a lorry driver, driving at night for Tesco. I really loved this work. I could be on my own, I liked my own company and the money was reasonable. Looking back, it surprises me how much I really did like to be on my own. To be honest, I felt uncomfortable being with other people; I felt I had to pretend and be somebody I wasn't. In any case, who was I? Apart from Cam, nobody really knew me. They only saw the side of me I wanted them to see; the rest was well and truly hidden, the pain and anger caused by my father masked by drugs.

Before long Cam found another job at a night club in Nottingham and, just like before, I worked as a barmaid and then as a podium dancer. It was great fun. I could wear what I wanted, take drugs, dance all night and get paid for it! Mind you, I was still driving lorries for the agency, and for a while life seemed a little hectic – there just weren't enough nights in the week to fit in all the work! So I cut back on the driving. By this time Ian left us to move to Brighton, and before long Cam was offered a DJing job in Manchester. They didn't need any more dancers at this club so I returned to driving lorries.

It was July 1995. Between us we were earning a lot of money. But we also spent a lot. Cam was having a measure of success with Vertigo in Zark Porter's studio, the same recording studio the World Wide Message Tribe were using. It was bizarre really: between recording sessions the two groups would meet and they'd end up having conversations about the meaning of life. At the same time I was taking more and more acid and Cam was mixing speed with drink. But in case it sounds as though we were gliding through life feeling permanently happy, we weren't. By the end of the night, after I'd been driving and he'd been working, I'd go and pick him up and it wasn't long before we'd end up arguing about something. He would be tired and coming down and I would still be on an up. Ian came back to live with us again after losing his job in Brighton, so we often went out together after work, sometimes not getting home until after seven in the morning.

Despite our arguments, I thought life was quite reasonable. The drugs were blotting out all thoughts of my past and the aggravation of the past year. That was until I came down off the LSD; then I would sit up and watch the sun rise and feel the depression creep over me. I would put on my Goth music and think about death. Sometimes when I was driving the articulated lorries, I would fantasise about driving the lorry off a high bridge or putting my foot down to see what would happen with 40 tonnes behind me going downhill. How quickly would I die? Would I feel pain? Would I be instantly transported into another life? Would it be light or dark? Would there be other people there? Would God be there?

I thought about death a lot – there was part of me that longed to know what death felt like. Would it be the ultimate trip? What would happen to me after I'd died? Was there a God? Was there life after death? Was there such a place as hell? At times life and death seemed to merge; I felt as if I was moving from one to the other and back again, hovering between the two, not sure which state I preferred.

I started to really enjoy these times of thinking; I suppose they verged on fantasy. But yet these were questions that I was really interested in mulling over, so I guess they were questions that I really wanted answers to. It sounded a bit macabre sharing these thoughts with anybody else, even Cam. I thought he'd think I was really depressed if I talked about dying; in any case, he might think I didn't enjoy living with him, or want to marry him. I sometimes wondered if anybody else talked to themselves like I did.

Then something really strange happened. Cam went to church one night with Zark and came back beaming. I looked at him; his appearance had changed. It was as though there was a glow around him. He came into the flat bouncing off the walls, telling me Jesus had saved him and that God was true – he really did exist! What? Had he lost his head? Immediately I argued with him. What about all the suffering in the world? If God was there then why hadn't he protected me as a child? What was he talking about? And if there was a God, what sort of a God was he?

The next day I left him and went back to Scotland to spend a week with my parents. I realised that I loved Cam so much and I didn't want to fight him over what he believed. If God had become attractive to him then I had competition! And in any case, if God meant that much to him, I didn't want to stand in his way. It was better that I make myself scarce for a few days. And besides, I reasoned to myself that it might all be a passing phase. Give him a week and he would probably be back to the old Cam and life could continue as before.

I could not have been more wrong.

10

The most important
decision of my life

I tried everything I knew to put him off going to church – sex, drugs, nights spent in our favourite clubs with our friends. I could not cope with the new drug-free Cam. Suddenly our flat was full of his new friends, and what's more they would sit together and study the Bible! There would be Zark, Mark Pennells and Andy Hawthorne. I couldn't join in; they were talking another language. These were not people I understood. They were on another wavelength. In short, I didn't like them and I certainly didn't trust them.

When they first started, Ian and I would retreat to the kitchen with a bottle of Martini during these Bible study sessions. I told them I had washing to do! We thought it would only last a short time and then Cam would get fed up with his new friends and come back and join us. But he didn't get fed up. On the contrary, he became more and more enthusiastic and involved, convinced these people were on to something good. In desperation, I signed up for overtime driving the trucks just to get out of the flat. Ian and I hated it all and felt like strangers in our own flat.

Cam started to go to Planet Life and would drag me along. He started to go to church and would drag me there too. I began an Alpha-type course called Workout. The other people were all right but were too friendly and made me feel uncomfortable. I wanted space and I felt they were invading me! Everything within me wanted to run. But where would I go? Cam was changing so fast I hardly knew him – yet he was the same Cam that I loved and cared deeply for. It all felt uncanny and I felt unsure. I suppose I felt vulnerable that if these Christians found out about my past they might be shocked. And I didn't want to stop taking drugs. If I stopped taking drugs, I was frightened depression would overwhelm me. I definitely couldn't live without drugs, even if Cam had managed to kick the habit.

Cam was working for Kiss FM presenting the weekend breakfast shows as well as DJing at night. My lifestyle got wilder, rebelling against this squeaky-clean, drug-free Cam. I went to a couple of World Wide Message Tribe gigs but couldn't understand what they were talking or singing about, and I just didn't like it. It was as though I was impervious to their message: I could not relate to it or them. And I wasn't even indifferent; I felt hostile towards them.

The only light on the horizon was the Workout course; at least that began to answer some of my questions, but I still thought the people were too nice and not to be trusted.

I had a big problem with the whole notion of a 'Father God' and this Jesus guy and what he did. Particularly with God, it was the 'Father' bit. I had been betrayed by the man who was supposed to be the most important man in my life; the man who was supposed to teach me how to relate to the opposite sex; the man I was to look up to in life; and the man who was supposed to provide me with a role model when looking for a husband.

And my problem with Jesus? Well, he was God. How could he be a man and be God at the same time?

By now it was the end of November 1995. The Workout course was nearing its end and I found myself on an away day with the church. We were taken to a beautiful retreat centre in Didsbury. The idea was to get us out of our normal city environment to talk about what we had learnt on the course, and what we were going to do about it.

As the day drew to a close, the group met together in the chapel and a woman called Angie told her story. Much to my amazement she told how she had been abused by her father, but with the help of Jesus she could truthfully say the pain of that experience no longer hurt her. In fact, she went a step further than that and said that God had healed her hurt emotions and restored her to the person she was always meant to be – she felt complete. I didn't. I knew I was a wreck. I knew I was broken and beaten up inside.

During a time of communion I started to cry. I felt sad but at the same time comforted and safe. I hadn't felt that sort of comfort or safety before. The closest I had come to it was with Cam. But this was different. This was deeper and even better.

I wanted to tell Roger and Angie, the leaders of the Workout course, what had happened to me as a child. I didn't say too much, there wasn't time. But they got the message and prayed for me. I left that day feeling happy and relieved and later told Cam that I thought I had become a Christian. I really felt I had met God.

The next week I went to Planet Life and listened to Andy Hawthorne preach about God wanting us to be either hot or cold but not lukewarm. I decided that I couldn't be completely sold out for God, so I had better be cold. After that deliberate decision I went clubbing every night and started mixing my drugs: LSD with E and, when I had the money, Charlie. I left Cam to it. He had chosen to change track; I was going to stay where I was. His God was not for me. He was becoming more and more involved with the Tribe and going to church most of the time.

In the spring of 1996 Ian left us again. My life remained unchanged although God seemed to be around more; in fact he kept turning up! When I was away at night driving the trucks, I would often switch on the radio – and there he was! People would be chatting about God or talking about the meaning of life. I can remember one night in particular. I was driving down the M1 and noticed that somebody had written on a bridge 'Jesus'. On the next bridge it said, 'Jesus lives!'

I felt as though I just couldn't get away from him, yet he wasn't being invasive. He was just there! I started to believe in God again, but I didn't want to lose control of my life even though I wasn't really in control anyway! For me, at that time, the big danger in believing in God was letting a male figure be the focus of my life. It was crazy. That was the very thing I didn't want to do. I daren't do that.

Cam became even more involved with the Tribe and sometimes would do gigs with them in Holland, Norway and Germany. I can remember going to the airport to meet him one day. I was still up on whatever it was I'd been taking and he knew it. He gave me a knowing look and whisked me off before anybody could realise. I suppose he was wanting to protect me, waiting for me to catch up with him! On another occasion, after driving to the airport to meet him, when we got home I collapsed. We both knew that our lives were growing apart.

We couldn't carry on like this for much longer, and Cam was so sure that what he had found was worth keeping. I couldn't deny that. He was fulfilled. He was free from drugs. He was happy. He had good friends. He had everything he wanted. I was still searching and frightened to give up the lifestyle that I thought I enjoyed.

Then one day, Andy asked me to come to Spring Harvest (the Christian festival) at Skegness over the Easter weekend.

He told me Cam was going. I dug my heels in. No way was I going to spend Easter at some Christian knees-up! When Andy pressed me about it and asked me why I wasn't going, I told him it was because the gay village would be open twenty-four hours over the Easter weekend and that's where I intended to go and enjoy myself. I don't think he was too happy! My only concession was that I would join them for a couple of days after Easter.

So Cam went off to Spring Harvest and I went with my friends to the Paradise Factory. It was a strange weekend. I was dancing with others and a guy asked me if I would like a job as a dancer/greeter in a new night club called the Temple in Bolton. I agreed and promised to contact him later that week. From the Paradise Factory we made our way to the Breakfast Club, which ran from 3 a.m. to 7 a.m., and then on to Danceteria, which finished at noon.

The next night I was out again doing exactly the same things as I'd been doing the night before. But something was different. I felt different. I felt as if God was talking to me, inviting me to try him and then see how I felt about him. I really couldn't enjoy myself that night. I knew it wasn't the drugs, because they had never affected me in this way before. It's true they made me do things and go to places that I wouldn't otherwise have done. On drugs I didn't care about my safety; to be honest, I'm amazed that I'm still alive. I knew I had to make some serious decisions. Was I going to take that job at the Temple? If I took that job I'd be out at least four nights every week and I'd be taking more drugs, which meant I probably wouldn't be able to live with Cam any more.

So, with very mixed feelings, I went to Spring Harvest. The first night was bearable. I didn't really engage with what was going on. I think my head was so full of thoughts, and I was probably still coming down from all the drugs I'd been taking over Easter. But the next morning was awful – everybody had a smile on their face. Everybody! The closer I looked the more apparent it became. I was with hundreds and hundreds of happy people. And they were hugging each other! It reminded me of the film about the Stepford Wives. This is a movie where men move into a community with their wives to work for the same company. The company takes the wife and replaces her with a replica robot which smiles all the time and bakes bread. It just felt as if everyone at Spring Harvest was brainwashed. It was all too happy for my liking.

Well, that day I reluctantly went to the events the Tribe were doing and I hated every minute of it. In the evening I slipped away with Cam and a few of his friends and found myself in the Big Top for the main evening meeting. The speaker was talking about the hurts and betrayals of our fathers and past generations and how Jesus came to take the pain and the punishment for them. It just clicked! It was the first talk that I had really listened to, and certainly the first talk that I had understood and could relate to. At the end, he asked for people to stand up if they wanted to respond to God. Before I knew it I was on my feet, and the peace I felt was indescribable.

'Try me,' God had said. 'Try me before deciding whether or not you want to reject me and live your life on your own.' That night I tried him and I knew I had found what I was looking for. I can't explain it, but I also knew that I could trust God. Yes, he stood as a male figurehead. But in that moment, that wasn't a problem. I was too delighted to have found him. The other problems and questions I had been asking still merited answers. But they were no obstacle for me in accepting Jesus that night. I still have difficulty articulating just what it was that the speaker said that night that persuaded me; but I was listening and looking for a solution as to which direction my life was to go. Was I to believe in God and risk letting go of my current lifestyle, or was I to carry on and take the job at the Temple? Somehow the decision was important. I was choosing a lifestyle. And it was a stark choice. Either I could go further into my life with drugs, or I could try God and discover whether he could help me to recover from the abuse I'd suffered all my life.

I went straight from that meeting to find the Tribe, who were about to pray before going on stage. I saw Andy and Mark and gave them a hug. They were gobsmacked! I had never shown them any affection before, only hostility. In fact I had hated them passionately. After all, from where I stood, they had taken Cam away from me. But now all that had changed. I am so grateful that they didn't bear grudges because they embraced me back and were so welcoming and accepting. I prayed my first prayer with them that night. Andy was so happy he jumped on to the table in the dressing room, whereupon it snapped off the wall! The manager understood.

Immediately our lives changed, and without us even talking about it Cam and I knew that as Christians we could no longer sleep together until we were married. So that night Cam moved on to the couch bed, which was hard for both of us.

But God had encouraged me to try him and let him show me how he could help me; and that would involve changes in my life. Many were obvious, and it surprised me how quickly my thinking and attitude altered. The deeper problems would take time, and I was eager to see how God would solve these. It was a case of taking a step at a time. I wasn't on my own. The Tribe were great. They had been very accepting of Cam, and doubtless the prayer that had gone up for me had been intense! But here I was. I had taken that decision; the most important decision of my life.

11

The wedding

My next challenge was to survive Soul Survivor 1996. By this time I had started to make some Christian friends: people like Beth (now Beth Redman), Loretta (a member of the Christian pop band Shine) and Sophie. I can remember going to a seminar with them to hear Mary Pytches speaking on the subject of 'Father God'. She was comparing God the Father with biological fathers – the two could be very different! She described the ideal of fatherhood in ways which made me realise afresh just what a lousy father I had. She also talked about how important it was to forgive our biological fathers if we held anything against them, because this was what God wanted us to do in order that we could be free from the painful effects of our past. This challenged me, and I found it hard to listen to, let alone agree with, because of the issue of forgiveness. You see, I still felt the victim. After all, I had not asked my father to abuse me. I felt he had robbed me of my childhood and my innocence. My memories were all unhappy ones. I was the one who had been violated. Didn't I have every right to feel that I was the one who had been sinned against? I was the one who deserved an apology! So why should I be expected to forgive my father for what he had done to me?

I walked out. I couldn't listen to any more. Although I have since come to understand where she was coming from, I initially felt Mary Pytches didn't know what she was talking about. Surely my situation had to be an exception? Was she suggesting I was expected to forgive my father? I refused even to consider the issue. No way was my dad going to be let off by me forgiving him. I hated him so much. And I couldn't understand why God had allowed all this to happen to me. After all, if he was so powerful and all-knowing, then why didn't he do something to stop my father abusing me? Surely he saw how young and innocent I was as a little girl, when my father used to come into my bedroom, into my bed, and sexually abuse me? I felt angry and let down. All my life I'd been made to suffer for something that wasn't my fault; forgiveness certainly wasn't on my agenda.

But then I would read Psalm 139, and in some ways I'd find it helpful – the fact that God knew me before I was even conceived, that he had always loved me and been there for me. But in other ways it made me angry because he chose those parents for me.

My faith was very mixed up. I could relate to the Jesus side of God. Jesus was like a friend; he made sense. But I wasn't ready to have another father in my life.

I still went clubbing, but only occasionally now. I didn't take as many drugs, just the occasional wrap of wizz (amphetamines). I thought I wouldn't have the energy to dance all night if I didn't take something to keep me going. But I never took acid again. That would have been wrong in my eyes; I wouldn't have been in total control of my mind and I figured that wouldn't have been right to God. I didn't even drink much at this stage. It was just the occasional wizz that I managed to justify to myself.

I was getting to know Angie better by now. She became a

good friend and we read the Bible together and discussed all sorts of issues. She was a great support, and still is. She would say to me that God would help me to change those things in my life that he wanted to change in order that I might find a better way of life. She suggested that God might know better than me what I needed and his choice would be perfect; in fact, she even suggested that living by the plan that God had for my life would actually make me happy and I'd feel fulfilled.

Angie also reassured me that God would not hurry me. He would be gentle and would do things in his own time and in a way that I would find acceptable. In other words, God knew me, he knew what I'd been through and he understood what I needed in order to rebuild and reshape my life, and allow me to become the person he'd always intended me to be. This is when I really understood that I didn't have to change for God to love or accept me; he loved me already, as I was. In fact, he'd always loved me, even when I'd decided to turn cold towards him and ignore him. Before this revelation I thought that I had to stick by all the rules and get all the answers to all the questions correct before qualifying as a Christian. But as Angie explained how God saw me, I started to get a different perspective on my life. I realised then that I could do things at my (and God's) speed rather than try and please other people around me in the church, and try to achieve their expectations of me.

This was a moment of great revelation to me. It took a little while to sink in. But once I'd grasped the truth and reality of this amazing attitude that God has towards us, I was able to stop struggling with some of these big issues. I didn't need answers to all my questions in order to believe in God. I could believe in him and still have my questions, but ask him to show me the answers! Understanding and accepting this immediately took a lot of pressure off me. I didn't feel as though I was fighting the battle on my own. I didn't feel that I wasn't good enough for God; rather, I began to understand that in his kindness, and because he understands us human beings so well, he has come more than halfway to meet us. He makes us acceptable to him if we believe in Jesus.

Roger Sutton, one of my pastors, was a great help as well. I never felt condemned by him. He accepted me as I was; I felt he understood the pain I was feeling and he seemed to realise I was on a journey out of it. He could probably see better than I the road I was walking. To me, all this new ground was unfamiliar, and having to trust my life to God and open myself up to other people was hard at first. Of course, as I learnt to trust my new Christian friends, the process got easier. But I was used to being a loner. I had, after all, learnt to survive by bottling up my feelings. I had become very effective at hiding the real me and putting on a brave face. But as I thawed under God's love and the love and acceptance of my Christian friends I could feel my old attitudes gradually changing.

Roger used to use a phrase when he was preaching: 'If there is a God . . .' He would then ask the questions that we all wanted answers to. I often had doubts and questions, and to hear the preacher asking the questions that I too was asking was very comforting. Maybe he had his doubts too!

The leadership of the church never once told Cam and me to live in separate houses. I really feel now, looking back, that they protected us from people in the church who perhaps thought otherwise. I was sharing a house with Cam; he lived downstairs and I lived upstairs. Matt Wanstall and Simon Vickers lived in the house with us for a time. It must have looked funny, I suppose, but we were all Christians and trying to live right by God. It was a fun time. Simon moved out for a while. Cam joined the Tribe full time. Andy came round once a week and we all had a Bible study together. We felt we were exploring a new way of life, leaving our old habits and ways of thinking behind and moving into a radical new lifestyle with Jesus as our role model.

Then one day Andy asked me why I didn't want to get

married. He was getting worried about Cam being frustrated and sleeping downstairs. I liked Andy, and wasn't upset at him asking me this question; he had every right to, he was the leader of the Tribe! But I still had a hang-up about letting a man control my life; that's what I thought marriage would be like. I didn't have any experience of living within a normal family, and my idea of marriage was based on what I had seen my parents doing. My head told me that they were unusual, but alarm bells were ringing in my emotions. So once again I was being challenged to take a huge step of faith in believing that if I married Cam, our marriage could be different.

But there was another problem. I didn't want to have any children. I thought I would be a paranoid mother, especially if I had daughters. I had visions of having to watch Cam's every move to make sure he didn't abuse any little girls we might have. I was carrying a lot of baggage at this time.

As the weeks continued and stretched into months, life continued and we were getting along well together. Then one day Cam asked me if I wanted to carry on living just as good friends, or did I want to marry him? My first reaction was swift – I wanted us to carry on just as we were. The thought of getting married was too big and too final, and in any case how would we organise a wedding? Whom would we invite? My dad?

I thought about it. I talked to Angie about it. And eventually I came to the conclusion that I couldn't see myself with anyone else and I didn't want to lose Cam, so one night I said yes, let's get married.

It was November 1996 by this time and we looked in our diaries. The Tribe had so many bookings before Christmas there wasn't time to get married! So we set a date for 8 February 1997 and the wedding plans went ahead. I decided to ask my granny to walk me down the aisle, and she agreed. I decided not to invite my father, and he understood that if he came then the rest of the family would stay away; there was no choice.

Two weeks before the wedding I faced another challenge. Cam was DJing at a club in Holland and I went with him. When we arrived I couldn't get any wizz; how could I dance all night without any drugs to keep me going? I decided to dance anyway, and five hours later I was still going! I tried a new experiment: I focused on God when I was dancing and worshipped him – I believe that's why I was able to keep dancing. God showed me that I didn't need the drugs any more. It was perfect timing. I was away from my Christian friends. Cam was busy. I was alone with God, and without the pressure of any other human being around me I was able to concentrate on God and test him to see if I really could depend on him – and I could! And what's more, God didn't condemn me for even thinking about taking drugs that night: rather, he offered me an alternative. He is so gentle! He didn't scream in my ear, or turn his back on me. No, he was with me on that dance floor – we were dancing together that night in that night club! God is everywhere: you can't shock him, he knows everything, even what we're thinking. He knows what we need, and I realised then that his solutions to our needs are often so much better than our own ideas.

I was so pleased. I remembered a conversation I'd had some time before with Steve Cockram, who was the first Christian I met after Cam had become a Christian at a time when I was still very anti-God. I'd asked him if it was OK to take drugs and be a Christian. He said that if I asked God if he minded if I took some drugs every time I felt as though I needed to and he replied 'No,' then yes, it was OK. But I never had the courage to ask God that question; he had to show me. And in his own gentle, patient way he showed me that night.

When we returned to England the following weekend, Cam and I decided to be baptised. We wanted to be baptised at the same time, before the wedding. It was really wonderful. So two weeks before our wedding we were baptised together. In the days running up to the service I knew that I had to make a promise to God never to take drugs again. In my mind, being baptised was a public declaration that I loved and believed in Jesus. In my heart I knew I was committing my life to Jesus and I didn't want to be half-hearted about it. It was all or nothing. Either I could trust God or I couldn't. It was hot or cold. And I'd made the wrong decision once before. I felt grateful that God hadn't given up on me when I decided to go cold on him previously, and felt so thankful that he'd waited until I was ready to make this sort of commitment. My parents came to the service. I wanted them to see the change in me. I also knew that my dad would not be at the wedding, so this was a way of sharing the other really important event in my life at that time.

Ours was an unusual wedding for all sorts of reasons. We decided not to have a wedding present list. Instead we asked everyone if they would bring some food with them towards the buffet. It worked really well! We didn't have too many quiches or sausage rolls – in fact we ended up having the most wonderful feast. People were really generous.

I shall never forget that day: it was really special, the whole day. Considering that less than a year before I really hated the whole idea of Christianity and marriage, I now knew that this was one of the best things that could ever happen to me. I knew my life was on the up. It had completely changed. I started to really care about people, putting them first and not myself. I wanted to help people, and not just the people I liked. Now, I found myself wanting to help people that I had nothing in common with except Jesus. I cannot overemphasise the change in me – I surprised myself! I used to be such an angry person, hating the world and everything in it. Now I would find myself crying when I was watching pictures of orphans or starving children on television, whereas before I would have changed the channel or made a throw-away comment that their mothers should be on the pill.

I had a huge surprise when, a week after the wedding, my car broke down and needed a new engine. My father, being in the trade, said he would come and sort it out for me. He duly arrived and took it away to be mended. On his way out he hugged me and said that he really loved me and was sorry for anything he may have done that had hurt me, and was sorry for not being a good father. That's when I thought I might be on the way to forgiving him. My thinking was really changing!

If only the story could have ended there. But three weeks after the wedding I had a telephone call. I was horrified to hear that what had happened to me had also happened to my sister Dianne. For all these years she had kept her secret to herself, but on hearing about me and Elspeth she felt she too had to speak up.

I was really angry with my mother. I felt she must have known.

I listened in silence to Dianne's story. How Dad had started abusing her when she was seven, had raped her by the age of nine, and continued until she was sixteen or seventeen years old. Dianne told me everything that she had gone through, from the rapes to him blindfolding her and covering his penis in jam and putting it in her mouth and telling her to lick. On another occasion he picked her up from school with a specimen bottle. He asked her to give him a sample so he could test that she wasn't pregnant.

Dianne went on to tell me that my mother knew about all this. Dianne had written her a letter in 1994 and delivered it to her by hand, explaining that I was not lying as the same thing had happened to her. My mother had never told me this. In the letter Dianne said that she wanted to speak to us then and discuss what action we should take, but Mum didn't want this to happen, and the letter was ignored.

And so it was that, just three weeks into our married life,

our world was once again invaded by more disturbing revelations about my father. Just as my life seemed to be calming down and I was starting to have feelings of forgiveness and compassion towards him, I was confronted with Dianne's experience. When would this nightmare end?

12

Further allegations

When I heard Dianne's story I was horrified. Somehow it reinforced my own experience and made me acutely aware that I hadn't invented a version of events; I hadn't dreamt or imagined these things, they really had happened. If anything, it served to make me realise that my father was a dangerous man, ruthless in his pursuit of sexual gratification at the expense of his daughters' and others' integrity.

Dianne told me that in 1972, when my mother and father moved to West Calder, she and her brothers continued to visit at weekends and the abuse continued as before. She told me her story.

'One evening in December 1973, when Sheena and my father were sitting in their front room I went downstairs to talk to them. I really wanted to speak to my father and ask him why he was abusing me. I just sat there for about ten minutes, crying. He looked at me with horrible staring eyes, almost willing me not to say anything in front of Sheena – I'm sure he knew what was on my mind. After about ten or fifteen minutes Sheena took me upstairs and tried to get me to talk. I was so frightened, and in the end I just couldn't summon up the courage to tell her what was going on, and instead made some excuse that I was upset about not having enough money to buy Christmas presents for the family. My father was obviously very relieved, because the next morning he gave me a £10 note.

'Sometimes my dad and Sheena would take Tori, my youngest brother and me out in the car and we would go for walks in Almondell Country Park. On these occasions I remember feeling that it was nice to be part of a family, blocking out what was happening to me at night. These occasions, however, were very few and far between. Most of the time my father was very aloof. He was not the type of person I could feel at ease with. Life around him was always very formal. To this day he still describes himself as a Victorian father. During my teens I became very close to Sheena and found her easy to talk to. I was having a lot of problems getting on with my own mother and Sheena was always sympathetic and listened to me and gave me advice.

'The room I slept in at West Calder was in a wing about three-quarters of the way up the stairs. Sheena and I used to stand for ages at night on our way to bed, chatting. I actually tried to prolong these conversations, hoping that my father would get tired of waiting, go to bed and fall asleep. On one occasion I remember him being very angry with me for chatting for so long.

'By this stage in my life the abuse had almost become a way of life, an inevitability. I hated it but yet I accepted that my father did it to me. I didn't feel I could speak to anyone about it because, although I didn't like what he was doing to me, I didn't realise then that his behaviour was abnormal, yet I hated having this big secret. It never occurred to me that it was happening to other young girls in the world; I thought it only happened to me, which made it still more difficult to even contemplate discussing it with anyone.

'Around this time my father started taking me to Ingliston car auctions on a Monday evening. He would collect me from Parkgrove after tea and take me home again at nine o'clock. He had started buying and selling second-hand cars while still continuing with his photographic business. He normally arrived to pick me up in a Ford Transit van. On the way home from the auctions he would frequently stop somewhere near Ingliston in a quiet country lane and park off the road. Then he would take me into the back of the van and sexually abuse me. This happened on numerous occasions and continued for a few years. He used to give me pocket money, and when I started smoking he would give me cigarettes. Of course, he made it quite clear that in return he expected me to "co-operate" with him. I think he saw this as his way of paying for sex – he was virtually treating me like a prostitute!

'One evening when he took me back to Parkgrove we sat in the car outside the house. I spoke to him for the first time about what he was doing to me and told him that I had had enough. I was angry and let all my feelings out. I asked him if he was going to keep abusing me and then move on to Tori. I was quite confident, however, that he would never dare try it with my sister because, to me, Sheena seemed a very strong person and certainly seemed to be the one in charge of their relationship. I think my outburst quite surprised him because he went very quiet; it was as though he was just waiting for me to calm down.

'I left him and went indoors, hoping that he would leave me alone in future. But it made no difference and the abuse continued as though nothing had happened.

'During this time I had two or three boyfriends and found I didn't have too much of a problem with the opposite sex; I wasn't shy of men like some of my girlfriends were. I do remember, though, having feelings of guilt when I was kissing and cuddling my boyfriends and could never do so without thinking about what my father did to me. In my last year of school I had one particular boyfriend and became very attached to him. In fact I became very possessive towards him and he finished with me. I then met somebody else at a hotel where I worked part-time as a waitress. We went out together for about nine months or so, and it was with this boyfriend that I had my first sexual relationship (apart from my father). I remember pretending I was a virgin, although I don't think I was very convincing. It would have been easier just to tell him I was not a virgin, but that didn't occur to me at the time.

'I left school in 1975 with only two O levels. While I was waiting for my exam results I applied to a few insurance companies to do office work. One of them offered me a job on the basis that I would pass five O levels and I started work on 2 June 1975. By the time my results came through in August I was already established in my post and they kept me on regardless! I did, however, attend night school later that year and re-took two O levels, just to prove to myself that I wasn't completely stupid.

'I remember another boy who wanted me to go out with him. I was on my way home one evening after being at night school, and he was waiting outside the house. He told me he liked me and we went out together for six months. But the strange thing to me at that time was that he only ever wanted to kiss and cuddle. I couldn't understand what was wrong – why didn't he want to have sex with me, after all wasn't that what men wanted? Wasn't that normal? I thought he didn't like me very much and I can remember how I was always trying to get him to go further. Looking back now, because I was introduced to sex from such an early age, I was very promiscuous as a teenager.

'On two or three occasions, when I was sixteen or seventeen years old, my father took me down to the south of England on business. He was delivering transporters. He would book us into motels where we shared twin-bedded rooms. He also took me to race meetings at Croft in Darlington. On these occasions we stayed at the Croft Malloch Hotel, again in a twin-bedded room. It makes me feel very cheap and dirty looking back on those times.

'I had a friend called Linda who worked for the Gas Board, and the two of us spent a lot of time together. The highlight of our summers during our teenage years was going to Blackpool. Even though we were very close, I never told her about my secret. While I was away on one of these holidays, my father sent me some extra money and enclosed a poem he'd written which left me in no doubt that he was missing me and reminding me of what to expect when I returned home. I couldn't go anywhere without being reminded of the threat of my father. It was as though I could never escape for very long, although I longed to escape for ever.

'Back in Edinburgh, Linda and I used to go to Fagan's night club three or four nights a week. During this time I was not getting on with my mum. I used to stay out late at night and caused her a lot of worry. In fact, what I was doing was probably no worse than what any other teenager was doing at that time – going to parties and staying overnight with friends.

'But in June 1976 she decided to send me out to West Calder to stay with my father for a month. At that time the last train to West Calder from Edinburgh was ten o'clock, so she knew that I would not be able to stay out late at night.

'There was a girl I knew at work called Joan. She lived in West Calder and invited me to go out with her and her friends to the Regal, which was a converted picture hall and disco and night club. The Regal was open every Thursday evening for teenagers and I enjoyed going there. I made some new friends, including another girl called Helen.

'My initial stay of one month lengthened into two years. I still kept in touch with my mum and saw her at weekends. But it was difficult and I felt torn in two because both parents would ask me questions about the other, and my father continued to abuse me. He used to come into my room two or three nights a week.

'My mother asked me recently why I stayed with him if he was abusing me. My reply was that it didn't matter where I lived – he did it to me anyway! I used to lie awake at night knowing that he was going to come creeping into my room. It was awful. Sometimes I would pretend to be asleep but that didn't work. One night when he came to my room I had my period so he left me alone. I thought then that I had found a good method of preventing him from coming into my bed. So a few weeks later I tried that excuse again. However, he put his hand inside my pants and checked for himself. When he found I was lying he was very angry with me. There were times after this that it didn't matter whether I had my period or not – he just carried on.

'One evening when I was about seventeen years old he came into my room, and at this point I had just had enough. I struggled with him when he got into my bed and screamed – I wanted Sheena to hear me and come to see what was going on. However, that didn't happen. Instead he quickly got out of the bed and told me we were finished. I replied that I was glad and cried myself to sleep. But it didn't finish there; the abuse continued. It continued until November 1977 and then, strangely, stopped quite suddenly. However, it was about three or four weeks before it dawned on me that he had stopped coming to my room at night. I remember feeling so relieved. As the weeks and months went on it was obvious that it had stopped completely. He never spoke to me about it, nor I to him. I remember thinking then that this was something horrible that had happened to me all these years; but I told myself to put it to the back of my mind and do my best to get on with life.'

So it was that a week after all these revelations had surfaced I travelled up to Scotland to stay with Dianne. Elspeth, my mother's younger sister, was there as well. It's strange, really, we didn't talk in detail about what had happened to us; I don't think any of us could really handle the enormity of the situation. We talked about him and why we had never talked to each other before and why we all went back to their house to visit regularly. We had so many questions. We wondered what we should do now. What was the right thing to do? But perhaps the biggest question of all – was there anybody else in the family, or even outside the family, that he had abused?

I was so angry. Angry at him for everything he had done, and angry with myself for ever feeling sorry for him. We wondered by now how much he remembered, because he had become quite a heavy drinker. I also wondered how much my mother really knew. Finally, we decided that we would confront him. We wanted him to admit what he'd done to us and we wanted him to apologise to us.

So I phoned my mother and told her that the three of us had met to talk and that we now all knew about each other's experience at the hands of Dad. She didn't say much. Her response was 'I bet you had a lot to say'. I told her we would be coming to see her and Dad at the weekend.

It was March and the week before Easter. Cam and I drove up to Gretna and we met Dianne and her husband, and Elspeth. We went for a drink beforehand to help settle our nerves – although it didn't really work. We asked each other what we would do if he denied it. We weren't sure, but we had more or less decided that we didn't want to go to the police. After our previous experience, we wanted to contain the situation and try and deal with it ourselves. We were still desperately wanting a simple apology from him. I still think that if he had said sorry, certainly Dianne and I would have forgiven him and wouldn't have been forced to take the matter any further. Perhaps we were being naïve. But we had endured so many shocks, and this latest revelation about Dianne only served to make me more nervous.

We arrived at Luce and my mother opened the door. She gave Dianne and me a hug but asked why Elspeth was there. Our husbands waited alone in one room, whilst we were taken into the front room which, as usual, was full of antiques. This was the 'state room' of the house; the room where he would entertain the likes of his bank manager. We thought it strange to be here rather than the lounge where the family would normally sit.

We waited for ten minutes before he came into the room. He didn't say a word. We asked my mother to stay and listen. He sat down in his usual chair and then said, 'What can I do for you?'

We asked him to admit that he had abused all of us. He replied, 'You are the ones with the allegations – what am I supposed to have done?'

Dianne, perhaps because she was his eldest daughter, was really brave, and speaking in a very calm manner asked him to admit what he had done to her and the rest of us. He coldly replied that he had done nothing.

At this, I was outraged and called him a pervert; even if he had only thought of abusing us he was a pervert, never mind actually doing it.

My mother was very quiet and said nothing. She lit one cigarette after another. But we carried on despite her obvious disquiet; it was her usual pattern of behaviour to complain of a headache or become unwell in unpleasant and stressful situations.

Once again, Dianne asked him to admit he had raped her, me and Elspeth. The language got quite graphic – we wanted my mother to hear first-hand for herself what he had done to us. But he wouldn't say anything.

We tried again and again, pleading with him to just admit, just say the word, just say sorry. But we were wasting our time and eventually he shouted at us, yelling that the accusations were all in our minds. He accused me of telling lies. Regarding

Elspeth, he had a very different version of events. And as far as Dianne was concerned, well, she was over sixteen and therefore above the age of consent. We couldn't believe it.

There was nothing more to be said. We were incredulous and shocked. We got up to leave, and as we did so my mother picked up the chess set and threw it at him. He looked at her and asked her why she had done this to him. In an extreme state of agitation, she shouted to him that if he didn't apologise we were going to leave and there would be more trouble. She kept on throwing things at him and screaming at him. He ducked behind a chair to protect himself. But eventually, he got down on his knees and said he was sorry.

My mother shouted to him, 'Say you're sorry for abusing her,' and pointed to me.

He said, 'Sorry.'

We left after that. We went to a hotel in Lockerbie to talk. As we told our husbands what had happened they became very angry. We were all upset, but I suppose it was expecting too much after all this time for him to do the decent thing and apologise properly. We couldn't make up our minds what to do. We didn't want to be responsible for sending him to jail; but we didn't want him to get away with it, either. We knew we had to do something. There was no way that we were going to be able to live life as if nothing had happened. I regretted going back and playing happy families after the last time the case had been dropped. Things couldn't be the same again.

Elspeth asked each of us in turn what we should do, and we all felt we had no alternative other than to report the whole matter to the police. We all agreed that Dianne and Elspeth would go to Broxburn police station on their way home.

Later that night Dianne phoned me to say that she and Elspeth had indeed visited Broxburn police station. I told Cam. It was only a matter of time before the police would be knocking on our door. What was I to do now?

13

More surprises

As soon as I heard that the police had been informed of these new allegations against my father, I wondered what I should do. The difference now was that I was a Christian; and, apart from Cam, I was the only Born-again Christian in the family. I struggled with the whole idea of taking my father to court and wondered whether God would rather I just forgive him and walk away from the proceedings. I knew I had to forgive him but the pain was so great. I had been hurt so deeply by my father. He had violated my body, my mind and my spirit. He had wrecked my childhood, and I was left with memories that I was ashamed of.

When my mother heard that we had informed the police again, she wrote us all a letter saying that she was going to make sure all these matters concerning my dad were sorted out, and that she planned to leave him. And we all believed her. To us, it was as though she had suddenly seen the light and realised the truth and was determined to stand by us this time.

It wasn't long before we heard that the police had visited

the house and arrested my father. He was taken to the nearest police station for questioning where, it transpired, he denied most of the accusations brought against him. He did, however, admit to having had a 'sexual relationship' with Dianne, but insisted that he had not had sex with her until she was sixteen years old (the age of consent).

I think he thought he would be believed and I think he thought that because Dianne was over the age of consent, he would get away with it. But this was to prove his first big mistake in trying to prove his innocence. While searching the house the police discovered his safe. There he had hidden photocopies of my diary and letters that he had sent to me when I was away at school. They also discovered a copy of the admission of guilt that he had signed when I had agreed to drop the case originally.

I was feeling apprehensive. While I knew in my head that the chances of us being believed by the police were good, I was still afraid that my dad would find a way of twisting events to work against us once again. We were so accustomed to being told that we had imagined that he'd abused us. We had lived with lies and secrets for years, and the fact that now these lies were coming out into the open felt strange and unfamiliar. I suppose it's like breaking any old pattern of thinking or behaviour, it takes time for the changes to dawn on us. There's always comfort and security in the familiar, however awful that may be. We'd been beaten down so many times, how could we be confident that this time would be different? And would we all stay strong and united this time? Already my mother was showing signs of wavering and siding with Dad.

It wasn't long before the police came to see me. They had my original statement, but now they wanted to see if I could remember anything new that they could use as evidence against my father. The police had been making their own enquiries, and by this time we had found out about my cousin Karen's experience. Apparently my father had touched her breasts when she was about thirteen years old. These fresh allegations concerned me, and the question kept arising in my mind of how many more people there might be involved in this tangled web of secrets.

As the investigation continued, the police were very understanding and I appreciated the way they treated us. I felt they believed us and were concerned that this time we go forward with the litigation. With my father already admitting to one of the charges, they told us that the case could come to court within the year. So we co-operated fully with the police and told them as much as we could remember. I suppose there was still part of us that would have preferred not to go to court, but it seemed we had no option. Dad was clearly not going to apologise; he didn't even seem prepared to admit he'd done anything wrong. This posed a real dilemma, and going to court was still something we would have preferred not to have to do.

Who, despite the awfulness of the case, wants to be seen taking their own father to court? Wouldn't most people prefer to keep their most shameful secrets hidden from public gaze and scrutiny? I'd lived with the secrets – could I live with the publicity that would inevitably arise from a court case? Did I want the whole world knowing what we had been subjected to – the humiliation, the violation, the indignity? Did I really want our story printed in the national papers?

I have heard it said that holocaust victims and victims of child sexual abuse have much in common; there's not much left to take when your body has been savagely brutalised and your integrity violated to the point where only your spirit remains intact. I have listened as holocaust survivors have described how they stood naked, starving, beaten, fearful and humiliated before their Nazi guards, yet indomitable in their spirit. I feel I can understand that depth of suffering. And I don't say that lightly. But for a child to be raped, thrust naked on to a bed, have a man thrust his penis into her undeveloped vagina against her will, endure searing pain, fear for her life, all this for years and years, night after night, by the man who is meant to be her protector, in a building called home . . . yes, I can listen in silence to survivors of the holocaust and, without saying a word, look them in the eye and empathise with the savagery and brutality of their experience.

On the way home I went to see my mother. I pleaded with her to tell the truth and stand by her daughter. She was clearly extremely annoyed with her sister Elspeth and also Dianne for what she considered to be their complicity in the case. To this day I don't know how long she had guessed or even known that my father had abused them too. Try as I might, I could not get my mother to agree to give me her word that she was prepared to support me, her own flesh and blood. It would have been such a comfort to hear that she, at least, believed us. Somehow her rejection of us, in favour of standing by my father when the evidence seemed over-whelmingly against him, was extremely hurtful, and made me feel as though I had no parents at all. She didn't say much about Dad and was clearly of the impression that if she didn't say anything or get involved then it would all go away! There was a reluctance in her to talk. She almost appeared uninterested. She certainly didn't appear to show any concern for us and the damage that we had suffered. She hated trouble and upset of any kind and had always gone out of her way to avoid it. I believe she thought that this latest storm would all blow over in time, and if she could keep her head down and remain impervious and ignore what was happening, it would go away.

It was like talking to a brick wall; my pleadings caused little reaction. She did eventually promise me that she would give a statement to the police, but I had little confidence in her determination to see my father brought to justice. And with that we parted and I returned home to be with Cam.

The World Wide Message Tribe were planning to tour America later in the summer. Michele Hawthorn, Nat Hanely and I were invited to join the band and go along for the ride. I thought it would be a welcome break from the impending court case. And besides, life had to carry on! The contrast was incredible; when I looked at the situation surrounding my father I saw only darkness and sorrow, but when I looked at the work the Tribe were involved in and the life of the Christians in my church, I saw light and hope and purpose. I felt involved in a mighty spiritual battle. If I looked too long at the darkness and evil surrounding my father I began to feel overwhelmed with despair; but when I looked at what the Christians around me were doing, when I joined in with their prayer times and touched on the goodness and the light that surrounded everything to do with God, then I felt there was hope and a way out of the confusion.

We (Michele, Nat and I) stayed in Nashville for some of the tour while the band flew to and fro across America performing at several events. This is when Michele and I started to get to know each other, and to this day I consider her a great friend. She would listen as I talked about what might happen to my father and my concern for my mother. She listened without giving advice, which I appreciated.

I phoned Dianne and Elspeth from Nashville to find out whether my mother had provided the police with a statement. Apparently she had, but I was saddened to hear that it leaned in favour of my father rather than us. The police obviously couldn't say much, but they did tell us that it did nothing to support our case and was more a statement in defence of herself.

It seemed that every step I took forward and every situation that I praised the Lord for, something would happen to knock me backwards. I really wanted to believe that everything was going to be all right in the end; I believe I had the faith in God for that. I wanted to believe that my mum would start to embrace the truth rather than hold on to the hope that her life could continue as it had always done. But I knew that because she was still living with my dad, and listening to his version of events, her mind would always be influenced by him. He was so much stronger than her in every way and she seemed completely under his control. He appeared to dominate her. My prayers were focusing on him telling the truth and us not having to go through with the court case. But in my heart I knew that his pride would not allow him to admit he'd ever done anything wrong.

He once represented himself in court against a charge of driving too fast, and he won the case. He had boasted about this for a long time afterwards and told us how clever he was. I could just hear him telling my mother that he would prove his innocence once again and she should just stay quiet and leave the talking to him. She was believing him still. How I longed for her to be out of his clutches and know the healing and freedom that I was beginning to find.

The tour over, we returned home to the constant ring of the telephone. Elspeth would call. Then Dianne. It was never-ending. We were constantly passing on new information, keeping each other up to date with developments, sharing our fears, the uncertainties, our questions, our doubts, our hopes. We were frequently upset. We were tense. Often the information would concern my mother. She insisted that she was not living with Dad, they were just sharing the same house but leading separate lives. We couldn't be sure she was telling us the truth. We didn't know whom she was loyal to. We reluctantly had to be careful that we didn't tell her anything that would jeopardise the case. We were involved in unravelling secrets that had remained hidden for years until now, and it was preoccupying all our time and thinking.

In August that year I went to the Soul Survivor festival as usual with Cam and Ian. Ian had become a Christian a few months earlier, in May. It was while we were away that I made an amazing discovery. I was pregnant.

We were so happy! As soon as I knew for sure I was pregnant, I went to a seminar that Mike Pilavachi was presenting on the Holy Spirit. He gave an inspired talk and then invited people to go forward if they would like prayer. I went forward and Mike prayed for me. He didn't know I was pregnant at this time. As he prayed, I sank to the floor under the power of the Holy Spirit. This was the first time this had happened to me. I had seen it happen to plenty of other people but now it was my turn! I had always thought that many people faked falling down when people laid hands on them, but here I was on the floor! I started to laugh. I couldn't move. It was as if God had his hands on my shoulders and wouldn't let me get up! I wasn't scared. It was good. I had a warm and happy feeling. Then I thought, 'Right, this is enough, it's time to get up.' But I couldn't get up. God was telling me to stay there. I realised that he was showing me and my cynical mind that he was working in my life, that people fall under the power of the Holy Spirit because he allows this type of phenomenon to happen in order to bring healing and peace. It was supernatural; I recognised that and so I stopped struggling and allowed God to do his work in me. I felt so peaceful and had the feeling that what was happening to me was for my good.

Eventually I got up. I sat quietly for a while, praying and thanking God for the child inside me and asking for forgiveness for the children I had got rid of. As soon as I had prayed this prayer of confession, I felt free from the guilt that had dogged me ever since those abortions. I hadn't known God then and it seemed that I had made the best decision at the time; certainly the best decision for me. But as soon as I realised what I had done and how wrong it was in God's sight, I felt bad about it and wanted God to forgive me. And as soon as I prayed that prayer of repentance, God took the pain and guilt away. I knew he'd forgiven me and I can honestly say that I have not felt guilty about it since then.

I can now look back on that day with hindsight. Now I understand a little more about the wonder of God's forgiveness, and when the Bible says, 'If we confess our sins he will forgive us', that's what it means and that's what he does. I think some people have a problem forgiving themselves. But for me, if God was willing to forgive me for all the wrong things I had done, then I am so grateful. And if he can forgive me, and he's God, then surely I must move on and forgive myself. Somebody once told me that to hold on to guilty feelings once God has forgiven you is to call God a liar. Well, I don't believe God is a liar. Satan is a liar and loves to hold us down with feelings of guilt. But with God we can have a new start, and that's what happened to me that day, and that is what has happened to many other people I've known.

After such an amazing time with the Holy Spirit I found I wanted to be on my own with God. So that afternoon I went to a quiet spot and sat down and prayed again. I started to pray in tongues for the first time. God really blessed me that day and for a while I even forgot about the family issues surrounding my father. I had a lightness in my spirit that I had not experienced before. This was quite unlike any experience that I'd had taking drugs. I knew this was real, and felt so special that God had come and found me, and talked to me, and reassured me, forgiven me and given me another baby. I felt loved by my Heavenly Father; he'd forgiven my past and shown me that I was precious to him and he cared about me; he wanted to make me happy! That gave me the confidence to believe that he would also help me through the difficult days that lay ahead with the impending court case.

Later that day, when Mike heard about the pregnancy, I was invited on to the main stage and I gave my testimony about how God had forgiven me and how I realised it was a miracle that I could still get pregnant after four abortions, years of sexual abuse and anorexia. It was the first time I'd spoken to so many people. It was the first time I was prepared to tell people I didn't know that I had been abused and I had abused, I had been forgiven and I was learning to forgive.

14

Days of transition

There was a part of me that wanted to stay at Soul Survivor that year. I had touched God in a way that felt new to me. He was transforming my life and I was starting to feel happy and much lighter in my spirit. I was beginning to believe that I did have a future, and what was even more amazing was realising how precious I was to God; he seemed to be going to so much trouble to make me feel special and loved!

I couldn't get over the wonder of being forgiven, and that wonder didn't go away. I didn't wake up in the morning with the sinking feeling that maybe I'd imagined it all. No, I knew something was different; I was definitely a different person. I felt like a new person, as though I'd been given another chance in life. You listen to other people describing this happening to them but until it happens to you it's difficult to imagine. But now it had happened to me!

I'd read in the Bible about being 'born again' and thought it was a rather strange way of describing things. But now I really felt 'born again'; I felt a new person with a new start. All of my old life had been erased and in God's eyes I was perfect.

However, I have to be honest and admit that I did have the odd moment of doubt, because when I started to think about my dad and the impending court case I sometimes felt as though I hadn't changed at all. If only I didn't have to admit to this. But I have to be honest and say that, while life suddenly was much better, I still had a tussle going on in my head sometimes. I had to watch my thought life. If I majored on the court case then I could easily start to wobble. If I majored on God and the events of the past couple of weeks, then it was wonderful – and still is! Of course, it wasn't through anything I'd done to make myself perfect. All I'd done was to say sorry to God for what I'd done wrong. He was so gentle with me, so willing to come more than halfway to meet me.

For a long time I could believe that God would die for another person, but not for me. And when I became pregnant, I can remember feeling that God would never forgive me for those abortions. But on that day at Soul Survivor, when God came to me, I knew he'd forgiven me: now he was healing me from all those years of misery, and now, because God had forgiven me, I didn't have to think about those abortions again – they were history.

So with mixed feelings we turned the car onto the main road and drove home. And for the next few days and weeks I felt closer to God than ever before.

However, I still had the court case looming ahead and that demanded attention. I had to come to terms with the fact that I needed to take action and face head on what was going to happen. I knew, deep down, that God would give me the strength to tackle anything and I believed that God would sort out this case, but I still had to go through the weeks, maybe months, of not knowing which way the trial would go.

It was weird; my life seemed to have two distinctly different sections to it. One section was my life here in Manchester with Cam, the Tribe, our church and all the Christians we knew. The other part was my past and my family. I would find myself on Sundays or at prayer meetings feeling so close to God, asking him to take all the pain and hassle away, for life to be normal and straightforward. Then I would speak to someone in my family and I would feel myself sinking down and getting trapped in all the negative emotions again.

I would get really cross and disappointed with myself when I allowed these negative thoughts to wind me up. But they did! And often! I would get upset with myself, thinking what a lousy Christian I was to let everything get to me. I told myself that I should be moving on, that I should be able to forgive my parents and not allow the past to affect me any longer. I would tell myself to focus on Jesus. So then, for a few hours, I would do what I told myself to do; I would focus on Jesus. And when I did that I discovered that I blocked out the other part of my life. I thought that was good and I was making progress until I came to realise that I was actually using Jesus as an excuse not to address the past. Deep down I was hoping that it might all go away and would gradually stop bothering me. You see, I was not facing up to it, and I began to realise that if I was going to let God help me then I had to be prepared to bring these two parts of my life together and gently let God tackle it with me.

For years I had been accustomed to dealing with these things in my own way, on my own. I had become adept at putting on a brave and cheerful front. I had learnt how to hide my true feelings and deny they were there. So when I met Jesus and he began to show me that I could be healed from all the effects of having been sexually abused, it was wonderful but unfamiliar! I had made myself vulnerable in the past only to be abused again, so learning to trust God was a slow process at first. But when I remembered that day at Soul Survivor, and relived those moments spent with God, I felt confident that he would complete the work he had started in me, and I also began to feel that I would be able to help other people who had suffered a similar fate to mine.

At first I would see-saw with the two halves of my life. One minute I would open up and feel a freedom to talk about my past and my concerns about the court case with my close friends; but then something would make me stop and I would turn my thoughts in the opposite direction and try and enjoy my pregnancy and my marriage. Christmas was approaching, and we were looking forward to seeing Ian and also Deronda K. Lewis (a member of the Tribe). But it was going to be the first Christmas that I hadn't seen my parents. One part of me wanted to go and visit them; but the other part of me knew that at last I had broken free from them and I should not invite trouble by returning just yet.

So that Christmas we sat at home and reflected over the past year and all that had happened to us. So many good things had happened and we had so much to look forward to. I found myself going over and over the good things, and suddenly I wondered whether I was in denial. After all, the trial was drawing ever closer. But it wasn't that I was deliberately only focusing on the positive side of my life, I decided that I was just redressing the balance and gaining some strength before the next round of major challenges demanded my response.

The start of 1998 found Cam and me in Switzerland. The Tribe were giving a gig on New Year's Eve. It was a good break and we all went skiing together.

So often in the past my experiences had dominated our conversations, and it was just wonderful to enjoy the moments when we were not talking about it all. Also, to be honest, it was hard for me to talk to Cam at times, because if I got too close to my past I would get angry and also very weepy. Until now, Cam and I had never sat down and discussed what my father actually did to me. I didn't know what Cam understood by the word 'abuse'; what went through his head when I used that word? There was a part of me that didn't want him to know in case he couldn't look at me in the same way again. I was scared that he would feel so repulsed that he wouldn't feel able to touch me again. Occasionally we would agree that I should tell him the full story, and at these times he admitted he didn't know how he would handle it so we never discussed it. My relationship with Cam was so precious to me that I didn't want to spoil what we were enjoying. So it seemed as though the kindest and most sensible option was to keep quiet. I talked to my sister, Dianne, and Elspeth and Karen understood – there was a bond between us, because of our shared experience, that was very strong. But they weren't Christians and sometimes I felt on my own even with them, because in some ways my thinking had changed compared with theirs.

Then suddenly, one morning Matt moved out, taking the studio with him, and Romani moved in. It was Easter Monday. I had been up till 1.30 a.m. listening to Cam's show on Radio 1, and then I awoke at 5 a.m. with painful stomach cramps. Cam drove me to the hospital, but by 8 a.m. we were back home. However, at 1 p.m. we found ourselves back at the hospital, and that night around 8 p.m. Romani was born. My friend Gail was our midwife; she very kindly came in on her day off just for us, and she was great! The first thing I said to Romani was 'Jesus loves you'. That was before I realised that she was a girl! I said, 'A *girl*?' I was convinced I was going to have a boy. Why would God give me a girl? Angie had boys. Dianne had boys. Why not me? But I knew he was saying that he trusted us and I was to trust him.

Ever since hearing that I was pregnant, I had harboured a secret fear that if I had a daughter she might be subject to the same abuse I had experienced. This was an irrational fear because I also knew that Cam was not like my father. But it just goes to show that old patterns of thinking die hard. In fact, I had convinced myself that God would give us a boy so that I wouldn't even have to worry about any daughter of mine being harmed. But I was to learn that God sometimes shows how complete his healing is by proving to us that our fears are unfounded.

This was when Cam and I really knew it was time to settle down, and we started to look for our own house. I felt I wanted some security now that I had a baby. We visited some estate agents and looked at a variety of properties and decided to buy a small house that we could comfortably afford, rather than burden ourselves with a large mortgage and have absolutely no life. We knew that Cam would be leaving the World Wide Message Tribe in 2000 and we couldn't be sure what our future held after that. We looked at one house and we knew it was right. I can only describe it as 'a God thing'; it had to be! The place stank of ammonia. Apparently the previous person had two dogs and three cats and they had stayed in the house – need I say more? But we knew it was the house for us.

After a few weeks the smell had gone and we moved in, and it felt good. The house needed a lot of work doing but that was fine; we were quite looking forward to making changes and decorating. After all, it was our first 'proper' home, and we loved being there.

By now it was June and Soul Survivor was coming round again. We hadn't heard much from the police and we were all getting rather anxious about the trial. We still didn't know when it would commence. I often talked to my sister on the phone and we would share our concerns. Those months were difficult at times; it was hard living with this uncertainty, not knowing when we would be called. It was as though life was on hold, waiting for the storm to pass.

Cam and I went to Soul Survivor with our new daughter. It was good to see old friends again and everybody was delighted to meet Romani. I spoke to Matt Redman a lot that year; he too had been abused as a child so we immediately empathised with each other. It's amazing when you meet somebody who has been through the same trauma as you. Somehow words don't matter; you just know what the other person has been through and it's that level of understanding that I find so helpful. I found myself asking a lot of questions about mothers to anybody I knew who had been through the same thing as me. My mother wasn't standing by me, and I was interested to find out if this was unusual. Matt was great and very understanding, but his mother had believed him and the family stood together.

To my sadness, I never met anyone with a mother like mine, although I've since found out it is quite common. I often wondered why she was staying with my father. Was she in denial? Or was she abused as a child and unable to cope with what was happening to her children? Did she not know what was going on? Or was she like the wife whose husband is having an affair; she's the last to find out although she has seen the tell-tale signs? Nobody seemed able to give me satisfactory answers to these questions.

So I went to listen to Mary Pytches again, and this time I went with Ian. I listened to her whole seminar and didn't once feel tempted to walk out as I'd done the previous year. She was describing the difference between the Spiritual Father and the human father. As I was listening intently to her, I was so in tune with what she was saying that I became aware she was speaking about me and my father. I felt sad but kept blocking the pain out in my customary way. I wanted to concentrate on every word she was saying and didn't want my mind to wander and start thinking about the past again. I decided to stay behind for prayer. It was as though I had reached another brick wall in my spirit, which I couldn't climb over in my own strength. I knew that only God could help me, and it needed his power in my life to help me sort out my thoughts about my father.

I stood as a lady prayed for the Holy Spirit to come and show me God's love and for him to heal me. I was crying and shaking because of the pain inside. I told the lady that I was going to have to testify in court against my parents in the next few weeks. I said it was important that I gave accurate and truthful evidence, that I felt I was needing to remember my past in order to testify in court, but at the same time I wanted God to heal me of the painful memories and help me to forget what had happened in the past. I was in a dilemma. She prayed silently for me and then said that she had to go. I don't really think she knew what to do with me. But as she prayed I did get a sense of being back at West Calder in my bedroom; it was night-time and very dark. It suddenly felt strangely familiar, except there was a difference this time – God was in the room with me. I suppose he had always been there and felt the pain with me.

It took me a while to get back to normal and gather myself after this, and I spent the afternoon with Romani while Cam was busy with the Tribe.

But something had happened after the morning session, because that night during the time of worship I really connected with God. The words I sang were not just words in my head: they were coming from my heart. I could feel the words now. My head was engaging with my heart and the words were coming from the deepest part of my being. It was the Holy Spirit clearing out some more of the blockage that had accumulated over the years – I felt a depth of freedom that I had not experienced before. Each time, God was healing me a little more; it was so reassuring.

We had a wonderful summer together, but as the days started to shorten once again we heard, in September 1998, that the court case would not be going ahead until the end of the year or maybe the beginning of the following year. How much longer could we live with this dark cloud of uncertainty hanging over us?

15

Facing the trial

So in September 1998 I was told to expect a telephone call
from the Procurator Fiscal's office. Apparently they wanted
me to go over the statement I had given to the police and add
anything I had subsequently remembered.

Just before this happened I had been reading – or to be
more accurate, I had been holding – my Bible when it fell
open at the Psalms. I read Psalm 25, and it spoke to me. Then
Psalm 26. Then Psalm 27. I found Psalm 27 and especially
verse 10 spoke to me very powerfully: 'Even though my father
and mother forsake me, the Lord will receive me.' I could
hardly believe what I was reading. It was as if those words had
been written just for me. I read them time and time again,
saying the words slowly over and over again to myself. 'Even
though my father and mother forsake me, the Lord will receive
me.' Yes, it was true, I did feel my mother and father had
abandoned me, but here God was telling me that he hadn't
abandoned me. Quite the reverse – he would *receive me*. In
other words, he would look after me in the days ahead. I wasn't
alone then and I wouldn't be alone in the future.

I was still glowing in the aftermath of reading those verses when the phone rang. After all these months of waiting it seemed that the trial was about to begin. The voice on the other end of the line told me not to worry, that everything was in order and was being taken care of, and we'd soon be hearing about the date for the trial.

I deliberately tried to keep in touch with my mother at this time. I was still hoping that she, of all people, would come across to our way of thinking and distinguish truth from fiction. I could tell she was having a tussle in her own mind; if my father was found guilty, her reputation would be sullied as well. Society had no respect for a man who had been found guilty of sexually abusing children. To be the wife of that man, and the mother of his daughter, living in the same house while the abuse was going on, was not a favourable position to be in. I felt that unless she stood by us rather than standing by her husband, the abuser, she would lose what little reputation she had left and lose any sympathy her friends and family had for her. All this time, despite indications to the contrary, I was hoping and praying, for her sake as well as ours, that she would do the right thing.

Then, finally, the news that we had all been waiting for. We were given a date for the trial. It felt strange. After months of knowing there would be a trial sometime, here it was. Reality at last. But two days before it was due to start, we received another call telling us the trial had been delayed. We had raised our hopes only to have them dashed again. It wasn't just the mental preparation, I had to think about Cam and Romani as well. The case was to be held in Edinburgh, and we lived in Manchester. However, we put this inconvenience behind us, expecting that the delay would be short-lived and we'd soon be back on track. Little did we realise then that altogether we would receive approximately ten different dates for the trial. Each time we would think this would be for real and we would prepare ourselves, get ourselves thinking positively, build all our strength up. Each time it was postponed I would feel very anxious and ask for prayer. Then as each new date approached I would feel ready and calm, only to receive another telephone call two days before the date of the trial to say it had been postponed yet again. This was torture, and what made it worse was not knowing exactly why these delays were happening. It felt ominous.

We were told on each occasion that the delay was caused by other more important cases being given priority; but we discovered later it was because my father's legal team kept applying for extensions in order to prepare their defence. On one occasion I was all set to leave for Scotland, but the day before I was due to leave our home in Manchester we received a call to say the trial had been delayed again. It was a nightmare – like riding a roller coaster. But I went up to Scotland anyway to visit my grandmother.

I tried to maintain a calm and regular routine for the sake of Romani, but it was hard; the trial seemed to cast a long shadow over our lives. And then we had another surprise. It was on Romani's first birthday, in April 1999, that I discovered I was pregnant again. We were happy but scared of what the stress of the trial on me could do to the baby. Once again I asked for prayer from my close Christian friends, and I was given 'words of encouragement' by some. To be honest, I didn't always find these helpful and sometimes even found them harsh. I was told on one occasion that we were here to suffer like Christ. I suppose that's true, but it wasn't what I needed to hear at that particular time. That experience has made me very cautious about giving 'words' to people. How damaging those words can be if we claim they are from God but all the time they are from our own imagination. It's so easy to say, 'The Lord says . . .' It can make us sound super-spiritual; but if those words are not from God they can do more harm than good. My experience of God shows that when he speaks to me, his words bring comfort and healing. Yes, he challenges me, but not in a sadistic, unkind way, and always his challenges come in the form of questions to encourage me to look in the right direction when perhaps I've been concentrating on the wrong issues.

The irony was, my parents had caused all this pain, and in times of pain all you want is your parents' support and affirmation. Marriage is supposed to be about two people leaving their parents and becoming one new and separate unit ('becoming one flesh' is how the Bible puts it); but at times I felt my parents were getting in the way of Cam and me. I was married to Cam but it often felt as though we weren't alone. I sometimes used to think that they would have liked our marriage to fail. I don't know if that's true because I never asked them, but that's certainly the impression I have. I have since talked to other people and found this to be their experience too. Marriage is an ideal that the majority of us want to achieve even if we've had poor role models in our own parents' marriage. How sad it is when parents don't give their own children the chance of achieving something they have never attained for themselves. I don't understand that attitude. It seems mean in the extreme. The contrast between my Father in heaven and my earthly parents is unbelievable! I still can't get over the wonder of realising how much my heavenly Father loves me and cares for me. I think many of us find that hard to believe at first, especially when we're not used to being loved and cherished by our own parents. I can certainly identify with people who feel that way.

Life bumped along, and two weeks before the next date we'd been given for the trial I received a message from my church; apparently my Aunt Josephine (my father's sister) had called them. I was surprised. I was told she had spoken to one of the pastors and asked him why I wanted revenge on my father and what were they, the church, teaching me? As soon as I heard about this, I rang her to find out what was going on. She wanted me to drop the case, and instead allow her to sort things out. She thought that if she told him off that would please us; she wanted me to agree to her having a word with my father on our behalf. I think she was trying to prevent the family's name from being dragged through the courts and muddied. But I told her he'd had plenty of time to apologise: now it was time for justice to take its turn, and even if I was prepared to drop all charges, there were by now seven other witnesses prepared to give evidence against my father.

She didn't say much after that; there wasn't a lot she could say. By this time the evidence against my father was piling up and the police were pressing for the case to start. I later found out that she was to be a witness for my father. To think, at first, I thought she was concerned for me; I was soon to find out how wrong I was.

The new date was set for Friday 18 June 1999. Cam, Romani and I decided to have a few days' holiday together before the trial so we took the ferry across to the Isle of Mull, where our friends have a converted church. It was the ideal place to be. Our friends Andy and Michele were also there with their kids, so we joined them for a while and then when they left we had the place to ourselves. Those few days gave us time to be together and be quiet before being plunged into a trial, the outcome of which none of us could guess.

As we walked and talked, I enjoyed being with Cam and Romani. It was a good time even though I knew in a few days I would have to relive my past again. Now and again I would be overcome with dread, and in those moments I sat in Cam's arms, and he held me tight as I cried. During our last night on the island, I woke suddenly. The awful reality of having to return to the mainland gripped me. I clung to Cam, telling him how scared I was. He was great. He was strong for me, and prayed for me and reassured me. I was filled with sorrow for him, that he had to go through this with me. We had only been married for a short time, and now that he was a father, too, this seemed an awful experience for him to have to go through.

But the next morning we had to leave the island. I didn't want to go. When we reached the mainland we drove to Elspeth's house. It was strange; I felt as though I was watching a programme on the television. Surely this couldn't be happening to me. It didn't feel real. I was trying to be happy for Romani's sake, but inside I was so nervous that I wanted to go and sit in a corner and cry.

We were almost halfway to Edinburgh when the phone rang. It was off! The trial had been delayed yet again. It had been moved to Monday or possibly Tuesday of the following week. We couldn't believe it. *Again!* We didn't know what to say. On the one hand, we had become used to being disappointed; but we all knew that the trial would happen one day and we were, by now, ready and wanting to get on with it and get it out of the way – this business had been controlling our lives for too long.

I would have dearly loved us to turn the car round and return to Mull; there we would regain our peace and be well away from all this pressure. But we couldn't afford the cost of the ferry again. So we stayed with Elspeth over the weekend, where we were instantly embroiled in talking about the trial and wondering what had happened to allow a further delay.

And we weren't the only ones who were wondering. It seemed the whole of Edinburgh was talking about it. What was going to happen was the question that we kept trying to answer. Was my mother going to do the right thing? Would my father tell the truth?

But by now I'd had enough and found it impossible to cope with the pressure we were putting on ourselves by trying to guess the outcome. I couldn't handle it. I was getting frustrated and angry. It had been so peaceful on the Isle of Mull. I had been able to think and pray and cry alone with Cam without pressure from other people making matters worse. So that evening Cam and I went out for a meal. It was just great to get away from everyone for a while. Space! Monday came and we were told to be at court on the Tuesday morning. At last, I thought.

That night I couldn't sleep so I got out of bed and sat alone. All was still and quiet. Cam and Romani were asleep. I kept a vigil with God, and as I prayed silently my Bible was open. I kept reading about the armour of God described by the Apostle Paul in his letter to the Ephesians. I wasn't the only Christian to come under pressure, Paul knew what it was like to face an uncertain future, and I drew comfort from these verses which described how God would defend and protect me with his spiritual armour. I knew I was about to walk into the biggest spiritual battle of my life and I also knew that I could not fight it in my own strength. Then I thought about the trial of Jesus, and remembered that he had spent many hours in prayer before entering into the courtroom.

Jesus' trial had been a sham, a farce. But he had conducted himself with dignity and prepared himself in prayer beforehand. I was following in the footsteps of Jesus and Paul, and although I wasn't the person being accused, I felt as though I was more than just a witness at a trial; I felt as though my darkest secrets were about to be exposed to the world. But would the jury believe me?

When I was on my own like this with God, I discovered a calmness and peace that I find difficult to describe. It's as though I was suspended in his stillness, cocooned in his love, held in his arms for as long as I needed. And as I rested and settled and stayed there, so I absorbed his peace and calmness. It was just the opposite to being with the family; when we talked I got wound up and agitated. The result was I felt exhausted and my emotions would be all over the place. So that night, as I sat quietly in the arms of Jesus, I prayed that God would give me his justice and peace.

16

In court

The court case opened on Tuesday 22 June 1999. By this time I was four months pregnant. This was the day we'd been waiting for for years, and suddenly it was about to happen. We were all feeling nervous and, frankly, none of us wanted to be there. But after months of preparation, giving statements to the police, discussing endlessly between ourselves the possible outcome and effect on all our lives, the moment had come for us to testify in court.

When we arrived at court we were shown around. I think this was done to help us relax a little. The courtroom felt large and impersonal. The dock, empty now, would soon be the place where, one by one, we would have to stand and give evidence of a very personal nature against my father. We had all been wondering how the case would develop and how long it would last, what we'd be asked, and how much local as well as national attention it would attract in the press.

We were shown to our waiting room, and asked the clerk of the court to explain what would happen first. The first thing, he said, was the charges would be read out and my father would make his plea. Then, if he pleaded not guilty, we would be called to testify against him.

We sat ourselves down. None of us felt like talking. We were all feeling tense. We were told the case had started. We waited . . . for ever, it seemed. But eventually the clerk came back and said Dad had pleaded not guilty. Dianne was called to give evidence first. We asked the clerk if there were any other witnesses, but we were not allowed to know. I told the clerk that I didn't want anyone to mention that I was pregnant because I didn't want my parents to know. The only thing he could tell us was that my mother, who wasn't sitting with us in the waiting room, was a prosecution witness, but she was waiting outside with Aunt Josephine, my father's sister. This we thought was strange, but we were past being surprised at my mother's unpredictable behaviour.

So Dianne left the room where we were waiting together and took the stand first; they were hearing us in order of the severity of the charges. While she was away the rest of the prosecution witnesses (there were eight of us) had to wait, not knowing what was being said in the courtroom. It was agony. We just couldn't rest. We paced the floor, wondering what was going on. Our thoughts were on Dianne. Would she be all right? Would she be able to withstand the pressure? We were all nervous about having to take our turn.

Lunchtime came and we were told that my father's first wife, one of my brothers, Nicola (who worked for my father) and Granny were all free to leave; they would not be needed in court. Granny they would question later, but the judge and both legal teams had accepted the statements of the other three. This meant that they would not be cross-examined by the lawyers as the statement they had made to the police had been accepted as sufficient evidence.

This was a relief to them and good for us, too, because it meant the prosecution had accepted their statements without cross-examining them. Dianne's mother was to have been a character witness, describing her experience of what my father was like to live with. My brother had given a statement describing how he had walked into a room and discovered his father lying on top of Dianne when he was only five years old. He had also told the police about the time in 1987 when I had confided in him about being abused myself. This was vital information, as he mentioned Nicola and Steve being there at the time and hearing the conversation. (Steve later testified to not knowing anything, which I was very disappointed about. I always thought he valued our friendship, but clearly loyalty to my father as his employer carried more weight.)

During the lunch break we went to a local café. It was good to escape from the unreality of the courtroom situation to a more normal and friendly environment. As we left, I bumped straight into two good friends, Diarmuid and Siobhan; Diarmuid was studying in Manchester. It was great to see them – in fact I believe it was God who brought them along at that moment because they were able to pray for me. It was just what I needed, to see someone who understood the spiritual side of things and who could pray with me before I was called to give evidence.

After lunch Dianne was cross-examined. We hadn't seen her since earlier that morning; it was forbidden to meet until she had finished being questioned. But by mid-afternoon Dianne was finished and escorted out of the courtroom by the social worker who had been appointed to look after us, although she was still not allowed to join us in the waiting room. It all seemed so formal, which only added to the tension we were feeling.

Next it was my turn. I was taken out of the waiting room and led along the corridor to another room. Here I was kept waiting for about ten minutes. I was in a side room adjoining the main court. I felt nervous and anxious. I couldn't sit still. I was praying constantly: 'God, help me to remember, help me to be clear; be with me and protect me.' I also was praying the passage from Ephesians chapter 6 and verse 10, which by now I knew almost by heart.

> Be strong with the Lord's mighty power. Put on all of God's armour so that you will be able to stand firm against all strategies and tricks of the Devil. For we are not fighting against people made of flesh and blood, but against those mighty powers of darkness who rule this world, and against wicked spirits in the heavenly realms.

I wanted to be protected from all the lies and the fear of my father and I wanted God to protect my unborn child.

Eventually I was called in. I said the oath and under my breath said, 'Amen'. I was praying in my head all the time. I was standing opposite the jury, with the judge to my left and my father to my right. On either side of him stood a policeman. The barrister was in between the jury and one of the policemen. Between me and the jury were the two legal teams, sat around a big table.

I vividly remember that the first thing that struck me, even before the questions started, was the atmosphere. Even now it scares me to think of it. I could feel the presence of evil spirits there. As I looked at where the legal teams were sitting around their large table, I could see a mist with swirling smoke moving to and fro between them and over them. I could feel a battle going on. I could feel the evil in the room, but at the same time I knew God was there. I looked at my father and he glared back at me over the rim of his glasses just like he used to do when I was a child, to frighten me. I felt nothing. I thought he looked pathetic. I looked at him again when I was asked to point him out, so he would know he had no control over me any more.

I was questioned by the Crown first and that went well. I felt comfortable with their questions and I felt I answered clearly and truthfully. Then I was asked to give detailed accounts of the abuse as it had happened in each house we had lived in, as well as the rape at Luce. This I found hard and I did get upset. Before my father's lawyers (the defence) could question me, the court was adjourned and I was reminded that I was still under oath. So ended our first day in court.

It was a strange and unsettled night. I didn't speak to anyone about the case, not even Cam. I didn't want the enemy to have any vantage points. I couldn't sleep that night so I crept out of bed and sat alone, reading my Bible and praying.

The next morning we all returned to the court for the second day of the trial. As soon as we arrived I was led into the waiting room adjoining the courtroom. When I went into the courtroom I was questioned by my father's barrister. Immediately he asked about Cam's name and questioned me as to why he had two names, and seemed to be implying that he was 'dodgy'. I told him that Cam and I had changed our names to Dante in June 1997 and even our passports and national insurance numbers carried our new name. But why had we changed our names, he wanted to know. I told him that I'd changed my name because I didn't want to be called by my father's name any more. And as Cam had been known as 'Cam' since he was eighteen, but had never legally changed his name before, he took this opportunity to officially change his name too.

'You are a born-again Christian?' the barrister asked me.

'I am a Christian. "Born again" just means that my past doesn't matter; when I became a Christian, then my life began again.'

'Your husband is the leader of a group of Christians who go into schools converting young people by taking them off into a room and making them say a prayer?'

'He is in a band that is invited into schools to take the Religious Education lessons for a week. They tell the children what it is like to be a Christian and answer any questions they might have. They explain what it says in the Bible, because a lot of kids don't know anything about Jesus and unless you know things how can you make a proper choice in life? They give a concert at the end of the week, in the school, and someone will talk at the end of the concert based on one of the stories from the Bible. Then they will say to the kids that if they want to know more or they feel like they want to become a Christian to stay behind, and then they chat with them and answer their questions. There is no pressure put on them; there is no point. You can't make someone live a life they don't want to.'

'All they do is go into schools and tell them about God?'

I was surprised he let me say so much about Jesus and was really wondering where this line of questioning was leading. I guessed he was trying to create the impression in the minds of the jury that Cam and I were members of some dangerous cult.

'Your husband takes heroin?'

'No.'

'He used to, then?'

'Yes, he has tried many drugs, but when he became a Christian he gave them all up.'

'He spins on his head . . . The church that you all go to has flashing lights?'

'No. Cam and I go to a Baptist church and the rest of the band go to various churches. Some come from a Methodist church background, others from a free church, and others go to an Anglican church; it's only a band, not a church.'

'You have ties with America?'

'Not that I know of – our church is called Altrincham Baptist Church.'

'What kind of Baptists?'

'Regular ones; part of the Baptist Union.'

Then the attack on me began.

'How many abortions have you had?'

'Four.'

'Four?'

'Yes.'

I had no idea how much he knew about me and I wanted to be as honest as possible.

He went on to suggest that my mind had been warped by drugs and that I was lying against my father because I wanted money from him to support Cam. He seemed to be implying that I had lots of boyfriends and that I was lying. He asked if I had said that David Browning (a friend of my father's) had tried to have sex with me, an allegation made by my Aunt Josephine. I said no. He asked me to read out cards that my father had kept, Father's Day cards and birthday cards. I got upset at this stage; I felt under attack. I cannot adequately describe in this book how it felt to hear the truth so seriously distorted. As far as I was concerned, he had obviously got these grotesque ideas from my parents and my aunt.

'Why did you send greetings cards to a man who was abusing you, who you say you hated?'

'It was the done thing. We all played along with the happy family ideal and I hated what he was doing, not him. I just wanted it to stop, I wanted a normal family.'

I was amazed that my father had kept all these cards. The police had found them in his safe, along with copies of letters from me at school and letters he had written to me at school, and also copies of my diary.

The barrister asked me to look at certain photos my father had taken of the family to prove we were happy. He asked me if my mother had met my daughter Romani. I said no, that while she was living with my father I would not risk taking Romani to their house.

He stated that I had not been in touch with my mother for a long time. I corrected him and told him that I had recently sent her a Mother's Day card.

He stated that I had not spoken to my 'close aunt' (his words, not mine) for a long time. I corrected him again, and told him that I had spoken to her two weeks ago. She had phoned me two weeks prior to the trial and asked if I could not see another way ahead; she had suggested that maybe she could have a word with my father, her brother. I had told her that all I wanted was justice, and as far as I was concerned the trial was about justice, not about revenge. I had also told her that we didn't know whether anyone outside the family had been abused by my father. She had asked if I was not able to forgive like other Christians, to which I replied that justice had to be done and be seen to be done.

The barrister went on to ask me why I was wanting to bring my father to trial. I replied, 'For the sake of justice and also so that he can get the help he needs and not be a danger ever again.'

'Where are you getting all these lies from?' I shouted at him. Then he said that he was sorry, and explained that it was his job to ask some difficult questions to make sure the truth was told. I felt betrayed, shocked and angry at what he was asking me. I knew in my heart that some of the things he was alluding to about my life had originated from my mother, because my father never really knew anything about me.

The barrister completed his cross-examination of me. His last statement was 'I put it to you that you are lying.'

I said, 'Why would I do that?'

He replied, 'Exactly!' and sat down.

The barrister for the Crown asked me, 'Was it not the case that even though the abuse was going on, you still loved your father and wanted a normal life?'

I said, 'Yes.'

By this time I was in tears. I was shown out of the court. I didn't know where to go. I was so upset, and had reached the stage of not being able to stop crying. I walked into my mother, who was with Aunt Josephine, and I shouted at them, 'I hope you can live with yourself.'

I left the courthouse and went across the road. I could

hardly see because of the tears. I was very conscious that I looked upset and that, being dressed in a suit, it was obvious I had been in court. I felt that everyone was looking at me.

Opposite the courthouse is St Giles' Cathedral. So I went in there and sat in a corner looking up at the stained glass window. I was sobbing. I was saying thanks to God but also asking him why all this had happened. It seemed so hard. And hearing all those insinuations about me in court . . . once again I found myself, the innocent one, having to prove my innocence in the face of fierce questioning. In that moment it all felt so unjust.

I made my way to the café downstairs and had a cup of coffee but I couldn't sit still. I phoned Cam and told him what had happened. He was looking after Romani and they had gone out for the day. He was shocked to hear how distressed I was and promised to phone the prayer team at Altrincham Baptist Church and ask them to pray for me.

I knew other prayer groups were praying for me. Women on Fire were praying, and Maranatha as well. It was such a comfort to know they were there supporting me in this way.

I went back over to the courthouse and met my uncle. He was looking for me, as he had heard I was very upset. I don't think anything could have prepared me for that morning in court. I had no idea it would be so awful. I suppose, in a way, I was hoping God would have protected me against such seemingly aggressive cross-examination. Instead of that, he helped me to get through it.

17

The case continues

I was with my uncle, having lunch in Deacon Brodie's, a pub next to the courthouse. We were sitting at a table in a corner facing the door, talking about the morning's happenings in court. Suddenly I noticed my mother with Aunt Josephine and my father; they had just come into the pub and were walking up to the bar. I wasn't sure if they had seen us, but it didn't take us long to realise whose side my mother was on. I had to finally reach the point in my thinking that I could not guarantee my mother's support in this case; she was obviously still hoping that the case would be dropped or my father would be found not guilty. We were on our own.

It was Elspeth's turn to give evidence, followed by my cousin Karen and then Granny. After Karen spoke the court was open to the public, so for the remainder of that day we could sit in and listen to the proceedings.

The following morning, Thursday 24 June 1999, at 10 a.m. my mother took the stand. Her attitude was very defensive and I felt that she came over as unloving and angry that she had been expected to give evidence. She had been called by the

Crown (our side) first. She said very little and spoke in very general terms, appearing to be unaware of the events as described by Dianne, Elspeth, Karen and me. She described her husband as a Victorian father – not very loving towards his children, more of a provider.

She didn't accept any of the allegations about Karen or me. She was asked if she ever left her or anybody else's children alone at home with her husband and she replied, 'No, never.' She was asked about Dianne having been left on her own with him. She replied that she couldn't recall whether or not this had ever happened, but couldn't see how or why she would ever have needed to do this; she implied that she was always at home and seldom had reason to go out in the evening. She said she couldn't recall the detail that Dianne had described regarding the events surrounding St Andrew's Night, when the house was empty except for her husband with his daughter, her step-daughter.

The Crown asked her why she would not leave children with her husband. She had no reply. I sat and cried quietly. Dianne and I held hands while she gave evidence. I just couldn't believe this was my own mother speaking. I felt as though she was kicking us in the teeth, as though he had stabbed us but now she was twisting the knife. Eventually I think I just went numb; or maybe it was God protecting me. I could hear what she was saying, but her words were no longer hurting me.

She was asked about the detail of the evening Elspeth was raped. She spoke about having escorted Elspeth downstairs to the basement where she was sleeping and said that then she went straight to bed. She said that her husband went to bed as well and she didn't think that he got up again until the morning, whereas he said that he didn't go to bed but stayed up listening to music, then went downstairs to Elspeth's bed. She was asked if Elspeth slept in the same bed that Dianne slept in when she stayed at the house. She replied, 'Yes.' In the morning when she got up, Elspeth had already left the house.

My mother said she was not surprised at this, as Elspeth always got up early to see to her horses. But she did say she was annoyed when she learned about what her husband did to Elspeth that night.

When asked to describe her daughter, I remember, she described me as 'a drama queen' who needed to have people around me. Our lawyer concluded his questioning by asking my mother whether it was correct that she didn't want to believe what had happened and that all she wanted was to remain living at Luce House. She agreed.

When she was questioned by my father's lawyer I thought she was very defensive with her answers – she didn't seem to understand who was who, and the tension of the situation caused her to become more stressed. She cried and asked his lawyer if he realised how upsetting it was to know you had grandchildren but not know how many or what their sexes were.

She said that she slept outside my room at night to prevent anything happening to me. I found that strange if she didn't know anything was going on in the first place. She said that I had told her about three times that my father had been abusing me, but because I retracted each time she didn't know what or who to believe.

When my father took the stand I thought he made a big issue about not wanting to swear the oath to God, saying he would rather make a promise to tell the truth. It was very odd; he made such a fuss about it I am sure the jury thought it strange. He said that he was an atheist but respected other people's opinions. No one else mentioned the oath and I was the only Christian witness that I knew of. As far as everybody else was concerned, it was just something you did.

As I watched his performance, it seemed to me that his whole attitude was that of a pompous, arrogant man who really believed he was the cleverest man in court. To me he was putting on an act which belied his true condition. He appeared to ooze self-confidence; I thought he could have been on stage. It was as though he realised his whole future depended on how well he performed in court. He talked about himself as a local employer, well thought of in the local community and a self-made man. He talked about us as a 'gaggle of women' plotting against him as though we were performing in a Shakespeare play. His barrister had to keep interrupting him, reminding him to stop giving speeches and just answer the questions he was being asked. But even after being warned by his barrister, his behaviour changed little. I felt embarrassed for him.

He was then asked to describe my character. He said he found me extremely frustrating. I was intelligent and could have done better academically. He described how I became very undisciplined and became involved with a rough crowd of people. He mentioned I went to Annan Academy and described how one day he was passing by a rhododendron bush in the estate and found my school uniform. Apparently I had hidden it under the bush and gone out in 'outlandish clothes'. He told the court he couldn't trust me; he described me as being very devious – not like himself, he preferred to be straightforward. He said that I didn't do well at boarding school. He was then asked about the 'incident' at my school. He said that I had written on a wall in a classroom for eleven-year-olds that I had been sexually abused by my father. He spoke about how distressing this must have been for the children coming into class the next morning. His lawyer asked if that incident had been resolved and forgotten; he replied, 'Yes.'

After a morning of watching him being questioned and cross-questioned, the court adjourned for lunch, reconvening as usual at 2.15 p.m.

Just before the court reconvened, I noticed he was sitting in the witness box, casually flicking through a photograph album which, we could see from the public gallery, contained various family photos. I knew exactly what he was doing. He was obviously reminding us that he still believed he had the power to intimidate us, as he had always done in the past.

At this stage his lawyer was still asking the questions.

Did he know about the abortions I had had? He said he knew nothing.

Did he know Sheena slept outside Tori's bedroom door? He said he didn't know about that.

He was then asked about his business. Was he grooming Tori to take over? 'Yes,' came the reply, as I was the only member of the family who worked for him.

He was asked about my husband, Cameron Dante. He replied that he had no time for Cameron because, in his opinion, he was exploiting me.

He was asked if I took drugs. He said he was sure I took drugs, and because of a recent television programme called *Everyman* which featured the World Wide Message Tribe, he drew the misguided conclusion that Cameron was still on drugs. So if he was on drugs then it was inevitable that I was on drugs too.

He was then asked if there was a considerable gap between his views and his daughter's views. To this he replied, 'Yes,' and added that in his opinion I was very undisciplined and devious, unlike him.

When he talked about me I felt he had real hate in his eyes and voice. It was as if he blamed me for the situation he now found himself in. He said relatively little about the others. But when he talked about me I got the distinct impression that he really despised me. I believe it was a spiritual battle that was being fought out in the courtroom that day.

While being questioned by the Crown he also waffled and was asked to stop. He said that we were a happy family and that we were lying if we said anything other than that. He accused me of lying because my mind was warped and I was after his money. Karen was misguided in her thinking because she fancied him. Dianne had forgotten her age, and Elspeth's judgement was marred because they had enjoyed a one night stand and she always wanted more.

When asked about whether or not he had abused us he denied all the accusations apart from the reference to Dianne. When asked if he had had a sexual relationship with her he said he had. He said she was sixteen at the time. He said she proved a willing partner and that with hindsight he regretted it now. We couldn't believe he thought the jury would accept his version of events and believe we had lied about the rest.

When cross-examined by our barrister he was asked what Shakespeare play he had been referring to. He said he couldn't remember the exact title of the play. When asked details about what he had done he got all flustered and could not answer quickly. I could see him struggling for reasons and excuses as to why he was innocent.

I had given evidence about the handkerchief that he always had with him and used to ejaculate into. I found out later that he had always made sure he had a handkerchief with him while he was with the others. He was asked if he used a condom while, in his words, he was 'having sex with Elspeth'. He said no, because he had a handkerchief that he carried in his top pocket. This was a vital piece of evidence and he dropped himself right in it.

His lawyer had asked him about the photo album he was looking at and asked the jury to look at certain photos to prove we were a happy family. The barrister for the Crown asked him whether or not he thought it strange that in all the photos showing him with his daughters, not one of us was smiling. He replied that he did have one picture of us smiling. But when he showed it to the court, he wasn't in the picture himself.

Having watched him give evidence, I was left thinking that he hadn't done himself any favours in the eyes of the jury. To me, this was the effort of a desperate man, trying to prove his innocence in the face of overwhelming evidence against him. But was I being over-optimistic? The case wasn't over yet.

18

The verdict

David Browning was called next. He was a friend of my father. He was asked, 'What type of man was Mr Forester-Smith?' He replied that, as far as he could tell, he was a caring father and a good provider; however, it would seem to him that Reginald's children were ungrateful. He went on to say how he and my father were similar, both self-made men. He went on to imply that he knew me better than my sister, and he considered me 'a bit of a tart'. He actually added that he didn't really know my sister at all. When asked what he thought about Reginald Forester-Smith admitting to a sexual relationship with his eldest daughter, David Browning said it was a lie. He was then told that Mr Forester-Smith had admitted to this charge. I noticed David Browning looked shocked and stunned when he heard this piece of information, and he responded by saying he could not believe it, but that if the lawyers said so then it must have been true. At this point in the trial, his whole expression changed and it was obvious to me that he didn't want to be there any more; he must have felt that if my father had admitted to this charge, there was little point in being seen to defend him further.

Next in the dock was my ex-boyfriend Steve. He was asked how long he'd had a relationship with me. 'Seven years' came the reply. Then he was asked if I had ever told him about these allegations against my father. 'No,' he replied.

I was stunned. I felt as though I had been hit in the stomach. I left the courtroom; I couldn't listen to any more. I went outside and walked into the pub next door and had a drink. I was hurt but also becoming numb because everybody seemed to be lying about me. My cousin came to find me to see if I was all right. I just couldn't believe that these people would deliberately lie against me, in favour of my father. What was going on? Never had I anticipated this would happen. Would the case end up going against me and the others? Would my father be declared innocent of these charges? Had we waited all these years and been through all this heartache for the truth to be denied and for the perpetrator of these terrible crimes to be let off and found not guilty?

The world suddenly seemed incredibly hostile and I felt as though I was the one having to prove my innocence. As I sat in that pub, I felt the whole world was against me; it was one of the darkest moments of my life.

Eventually I decided to go back into the courtroom. I left the pub and started to retrace my steps. As I approached the courthouse I saw my mother and Steve standing outside, talking to each other; it hurt me so much to think they had not stood by me.

I went back into the courtroom to hear my Aunt Josephine giving evidence. I'm not sure how much I'd missed, but as I sat down my father's barrister was asking her what I had said to her on the phone. She replied, 'She said that she didn't want to see her father in prison but she did want justice.'

That was the end. Dianne, Elspeth and I went for a walk and stopped at a café bar. We sat outside because it was such a sunny, warm day. We didn't have much to say to each other; I think we were all shocked at what we'd heard in court that day. A few minutes later my mother and Aunt Josephine walked past us. We said nothing; we had nothing to say.

So the next day, Friday, I went home to Manchester and the rest of the family went back to court to hear the closing arguments. The Crown's barrister explained again in detail exactly what my father had done to sexually abuse each of us.

Apparently while this was going on my mother sat in the gallery, her face showing no emotion. My father's barrister said that things like this happen in seemingly respectable families like ours. The Crown had to drop the charge of rape against me. They explained that they recognised he had raped me and that the jury would find him guilty, but because there was a big gap between the last rape of Dianne and myself, he would be able to appeal on a technicality and get his sentences reduced. I had no say in this because it was the police prosecuting him, not me. I was a little disappointed, but there was nothing more I could do; it was over as far as I was concerned.

The jury retired and came back on the Monday. They read out the charges and came back with the verdicts. They were nearly all unanimous, too.

Charges 1, 4 and 6
1 Shameless indecency between 03.10.67 and 25.12.77
4 Shameless indecency between 02.01.74 and 01.01.85
6 Shameless indecency between 01.11.79 and 21.02.82

Guilty

Charges 2 and 3
2 Assault and rape between 01.11.71 and 25.12.77
3 Unlawful sex and incest between 01.11.71 and 25.12.77

Guilty

Charge 5
5 Assault and rape between 02.01.82 and 01.01.84

Not guilty

Charge 7
7 Assault and rape between 01.09.71 and 30.09.71

Guilty

Charge 8
8 Lewd and indecent behaviour between 16.12.76 and 31.12.76

Guilty

My Aunt Josephine wanted to pay for his bail but he was told he would have to go to prison straight away. He seemed shocked.

The sentencing was to be in July, but it was moved to 13 August because they were waiting for the results of a medical assessment on him.

I started to see a counsellor because I could not get my head around being betrayed by my mother. I found this one of the hardest elements of the whole trial. I wanted to understand why she had behaved towards me in this way. Also, I felt guilty about my father being in prison.

The counsellor was very supportive and explained to me about sociopaths and how they were high flyers and often self-made men. They could appear very generous. They were sometimes eccentric. They were often thought of as good company. However, all these apparent attributes masked a very controlling, manipulative character, and if they wanted something they would get it no matter what the cost; they often appeared to have no conscience.

I immediately recognised all those personality traits in my father, although this cannot be proved and is only my opinion. But hearing this helped me to start coming to terms with the outcome of the trial. I felt that, however unfortunate for me, it was a case of me being the one who had been there, born at the wrong time to the wrong father. It wasn't a personal thing; it would have happened to somebody else in my shoes. That made me feel less guilty as well about him being in prison.

If the abuse had come from a friend of the family or an uncle, then I am sure the trauma of it all wouldn't have been so bad. Going through the trauma of the abuse was one thing, but to go through the trauma of the trial had brought it all back. I came to the conclusion that my father had made his own choices in life and had to face the consequences: it was not my fault and I had nothing to feel guilty about.

But my mother was another issue. At first I wanted to shout at her and shock her by telling her everything. But then, I reminded myself, she had already heard it all in court and it had done nothing to change her attitude. I wanted justice from her; I wanted her to admit he was wrong. I was shocked at her lack of emotion in court. And, above all, I wanted to know how much she had known beforehand and for how long. There was nothing my counsellor could say to make that issue any better; I had to find a way of coping for myself and coming to terms with this huge disappointment and sense of double loss.

I hadn't yet reached the stage of letting go. I desperately wanted her to phone me and say she was sorry that I had to go through everything on my own. I was disappointed in her, I felt she had rejected me and not believed me.

I only went for three counselling sessions to start with. I felt that some things were clearer, but then I reached the point of not wanting to talk about it. I was exhausted. Being pregnant and having a toddler and a husband was enough, but with all this going on in my head as well it was all too much. I had to close down for a while. My prayer life was pretty much non-existent. I could thank God that justice had been done but I had so much new pain inside me I felt as though I was hemmed in by a brick wall. I would ask him to take it all away, but everywhere I turned I could only see the brick wall. I felt as though one problem had been replaced by another.

It was Soul Survivor time again. We were going for three weeks this time. The Tribe were very busy with seminars and gigs. I had a real hard time trying to enter into the worship and be close to God. I would go to the meetings, but after a few minutes my mind would start wandering back to the events of the trial. I just seemed unable to concentrate on anything else for long. I think I was in some sort of shock. Certainly I felt as though my mind was going round and round in circles. Cam would tell friends about what I had been through, that most of the character attacks in court were directed at me. I do think it had something to do with me being a Christian and that it was a spiritual battle that was going on in that courtroom. Yes, things were suggested and said about the others, but I seemed to be in everyone's line of fire. Maybe I was worse than I remember being. I did get a sense that the defence witnesses were speaking about and concentrating on the 'old me' rather than the 'new'. Maybe if I hadn't become a Christian none of this would bother me. But having to sit and listen to all those lies had physically hurt me. I had wanted to say that the person they were describing was not me; I had changed. They had been talking about the old Tori. She was no more! It was as though they were describing another person. But I hadn't spoken to most of them for four years, so they only knew the old me.

I was glad to be at Soul Survivor surrounded by Christians even if I wasn't joining in most of the time. I spoke to Beth and Matt Redman a lot. I needed to speak to someone who had been through what I was going through, and had survived. Matt was a great help, a real encouragement. I was still constantly on the phone to Dianne, checking that she was all right.

August 13 arrived, the day of sentencing. I found myself wandering about in a daze. I took Romani to the crèche and then went into the morning meeting. But I couldn't get into it at all; my mind was somewhere else. I was sat clutching a mobile phone waiting for a call. Then Matt Redman stood up and gave his testimony about how he had been abused as a child by somebody very well known to him. I was in tears; this was too close to home. Michele was trying to be supportive but nothing and nobody could console me. I walked out, and then the phone rang. My father had been sentenced to seventeen years and three months in total, but the terms were to run concurrently so he was given a sentence of eight years, the consideration being that this was his first offence.

Charges 1, 4 and 6
1 Shameless indecency between 03.10.67 and 25.12.77
4 Shameless indecency between 02.01.74 and 01.01.85
6 Shameless indecency between 01.11.79 and 21.02.82

Guilty: 8 years

Charges 2 and 3
2 Assault and rape between 01.11.71 and 25.12.77
3 Unlawful sex and incest between 01.11.71 and 25.12.77

Guilty: 6 years

Charge 5
5 Assault and rape between 02.01.82 and 01.01.84

Not guilty

Charge 7
7 Assault and rape between 01.09.71 and 30.09.71

Guilty: 3 years

Charge 8
8 Lewd and indecent behaviour between 16.12.76 and 31.12.76

Guilty: 3 months

I was relieved that he had been sentenced for longer than five years because, to me, this meant he would serve two-thirds of the sentence, enough time to come to terms with what he had done, and maybe, just maybe, he would admit it to himself and then to others. We were safe for a while and guaranteed a few years of peace. I knew my father would be devastated at this result. I could only hope that in some way this sentence would bring him to his senses and make him realise what he'd done. I knew he described himself as an atheist, but my hope now was that his years in prison would give him time to think about God.

So it was over. But not really. This was only just the beginning of the next stage in this sad saga. That night the result of the trial was on the Scottish news and the next week it was in every paper: the *Glasgow Herald*, *The Scotsman*, the front pages of the *Sun*, the *Daily Record*, the *Daily Mail* and a few others. I was sent the press cuttings while at Soul Survivor. It was hard to see my father in handcuffs on the front cover of the tabloids. I would read the story, and it was as though I was reading about somebody else. It was a hard time. He was, after all, my father. But then I would remember those days in court; I would remember his attitude and the lies that were told. I would remember that he was not sorry for what he had done to us. And that made it easier to come to terms with this sentence. I am not sure whether I had forgiven him for the abuse by this time; everything was so painful and so many memories had been brought to the surface again. I would find myself feeling sorry for him one moment and angry at him the next. And I felt the same emotions for my mother. I wanted to be with her and close to her, but then realised that this was impossible; she too had made her own choices in life, just as he had done, and I was not responsible for them. I was only responsible for my attitude towards them.

Cam tried to get my mind away from the case but it was hard for him. I withdrew into myself and got very low. The rest of that time at Soul Survivor just seems a blur to me now. Something big always seems to happen to me when I'm there.

In November my father tried to win an appeal against his sentence, but it was thrown out. He had no grounds for appeal. That was a relief. Then, just as we thought we would have some peace, we were all sent forms to fill out so we could be notified about his release date, although we will only get three weeks' notice of this. I have since found out that he will be released from prison in 2004. I am dreading it in a way. I wonder what he will be like then. Will he have changed? Or will he be angry and intent on revenge? He doesn't frighten me any more; but I could do without any more hassle.

Just after the sentence was announced I read some verses in the book of Proverbs in the Bible,

A malicious man disguises himself with his lips but in his heart he harbours deceit. Though his speech is charming, do not believe him, for seven abominations fill his heart. His malice may be concealed by deception, but his wickedness will be exposed in the assembly.

(Proverbs 26:24–6)

It says it all. He had been exposed.

19

Victory or not?

'Business man jailed for eight years', ran the headline. 'A former society photographer who subjected three young girls to an ordeal of sexual abuse and indecently assaulted a woman was jailed for eight years on Friday. The High Court in Edinburgh heard that self-made businessman Reginald Forester-Smith's life was now in ruins after a jury convicted him of a catalogue of indecency offences and rape . . .'

'Man jailed over sex abuse on three girls.'

'Photographer in sex case jailed.'

'Pervert jailed for sex attacks on young girls.'

The headlines reminded us of the events in court and served to drive home the reality of the past few weeks. Life would never be the same again. Our secrets had now been revealed for all to hear and the media reported the results of the court case in detail.

After the sentencing, that was it. It was all over. We should have been happy, but I wasn't. If I had been testifying against a rapist whom I didn't know then maybe I would have felt a sense of relief. But all I was left with was a deep sense of sadness.

Of course I was relieved that we had won the case and happy it was all over, but now I had to face the fact that my father was in prison and I was partly responsible for putting him there. On the other hand he was totally responsible. He had made his own decisions over the years and he was responsible for his own actions.

However, I still felt guilty about him being locked away in prison and yet I knew I shouldn't feel that way. It must have been an awful shock for him because I really don't think he was expecting to lose the case. I am convinced he believed that, because people thought of him as an 'upright citizen', his reputation would safeguard him against the accusations. I cannot begin to imagine how he felt during his first few days in prison; I certainly don't think he would have prepared himself for such an eventuality.

The next stage we had to go through was the appeal. I had talked to the Crown and they reassured me he had no grounds for appeal. I felt a profound sense of loss; even though my parents were not like most 'normal' parents and I hadn't spoken to them for a while, I had to come to terms with the fact that things would never be the same again. I wouldn't be phoning my mother now and chatting to her or asking for advice, as other girls tell me they do with their mothers. I felt betrayed by her and deeply hurt. And I couldn't face up to all the emotions I had bubbling away inside me. I wanted to be strong for Romani, Cam and the baby I was carrying. I also wanted to believe that if I kept asking God to take away these emotions he would. But he didn't. I couldn't understand why at the time, and it was to be some while before I did.

Looking back, I can honestly say a lot of good came out of this episode in my life. I gained a sister that I knew I had but had never really bothered with before. For years Dianne and her brothers were kept apart from the rest of the family and we only really saw them at weekends for a few hours. They were much older than me and, after all, they belonged to my father's first wife. For years I was led to believe that all they wanted was his money; I was told they were not to be trusted and certainly not to be liked. Consequently I never made any real effort to get to know them at all. I was civil to them when they came to visit, but that was it. My father's comments were that his sons were both a disappointment and that Dianne could have done so much better for herself than she did (referring to her marriage).

Looking back, we can't be sure but it felt as though we were deliberately kept apart during the years when we were growing up and living at home. Dianne was sent abroad, then I was sent to Germany; maybe our father was worried that we would talk about him if we were given the chance. Now that I know Dianne and my brothers, I wish so much that I had known them more before; now, as a result of this court case, we are so close and they are such nice honest people. I love them dearly and greatly value our friendship.

We were all so supportive of each other through this time. Justice was done. We stood together and won. We had our freedom now; he could no longer terrorise us. But what would we do now? Did we have anything else in common? Would we always talk about the past? Now that the trial was over, would we revert to being aloof with each other? Would we drift apart again?

I am happy to say that hasn't happened. I think we've all discovered how much we love each other. That shared experience has definitely united us. Now, two years later, we do not talk about our past all the time. Quite the opposite – we are always pleased to see each other and share each other's lives. I really have gained my siblings back.

I do miss the intensity of those weeks and months before the trial. We were constantly on the phone to each other. We really needed each other's support, and we gave it – it was wonderful. Just to remind ourselves of that makes us realise today what great friends we are. It's true we are not phoning each other every day now, but maybe that is a good thing!

But in the immediate aftermath of the trial, I realised I had a deep sense of loss, as though there was nothing to unite us any more. In one way, it felt like an anti-climax. We had nothing to fight for any more. The thing that we had been focusing on for so long was now behind us. It had happened. It was past. What would I do with my life now? I had become accustomed to waking up every morning wondering what the outcome of the trial would be – in fact, for a long while I wondered whether we'd ever get as far as a trial. The court case had taken over my life and now I had to find something to replace it with. But what? My pain maybe? That was going to be hard to face and deal with. Or would I just bury it and try to ignore it, as I had done before?

I had been an abuse victim for most of my life and I never realised that I could change. For years I had suppressed my feelings and the effects on my mind by being angry. I had numbed the emotional pain by blocking it out with drink and drugs. But every time I sobered up I would get depressed and then angry again. It was a daily cycle. I had become used to living like that; in fact, I thought that was as good as life was going to get! Then when I met Angie I realised that I had the chance to change. I didn't have to be a victim any more: I could become a survivor. I hated labels but this one sounded better. I knew I didn't want my father to control me any more. It was true to say that he had stopped controlling me physically for some time; for some years I had been free to please myself. But I knew that he still controlled me emotionally. The effects were deep. They were a part of me. He affected nearly every part of my life. My moods, my trust, my self-esteem, my sex life, my eating, my nightmares, my self-confidence – I could go on and on. What he had done was not just sexual, it was mental abuse too. I had trunks full of rubbish, not just bags! But how was I going to change from being a victim to being a survivor?

As I have already described, I went to seminars and sermons and heard many talks on the subject of forgiveness. This was a word that made me furious, and it still does when the true meaning is not explained. All I ever heard was that in order for God to forgive you, you must forgive others. I felt forgiven for the things I had done wrong but I never felt pressure – well, pressure from God – to forgive my father. I knew if I wanted the best from God then I had to get rid of any blockages in my thinking, my hatred being the biggest. I knew that God understood me and knew I could not just forgive in an instant, that it was going to take time. Forgiveness to me, at first, meant saying that everything is OK, past and present. At first, I could say it in my head but I didn't feel it in my heart. I had a martyr complex! Well, it wasn't OK. It never could be OK, far from it. I knew I had to do something more than just say that everything was OK and it would be OK. What I really wanted was to let go of my anger because it was getting in the way of my everyday life. It was so near the surface of my emotions and it frightened me how easily it erupted. I wanted to move on and leave the past in the past, but how could I do that when it was staring me in my face all the time? Even if I didn't realise it, the past still controlled me.

The first thing I did was to shout at God. I blamed him for a lot of what had happened. 'Why did you not protect me?' I screamed at God.

The answer I got was that if he had protected me he would have had to take my father's free will away from him.

'*So?*' was my reply to that.

Then he would have to take the free will away from every bad person in the world for things to be equal for everyone.

Yes? The penny dropped. We all do bad things at some stage in our lives, so he would have to take all our free will away, and then would that be life?

I could follow God's reasoning up to a point, but he knew I still wasn't happy.

Every time I heard or read something about God knowing me before I was born and that I was part of his plan, it would stir up resentment in me towards him for where he placed me. I still sometimes question why God allows some things to happen and why all this had to happen to me or to anyone else.

I have today come to the conclusion that I just have to trust him. If I keep going over it again and again I will only stir up emotions that will eventually drive me mad. But if I believe that God is true, I have to accept all of him, not just the parts of him I find acceptable. For a time I found it convenient and comfortable just agreeing with the parts that suited me and not listening to the rest. But the truth is, God wants me to forgive my enemies and bless them. 'Dear friends, never avenge yourselves. Leave that to God. For it is written, "I will take vengeance; I will repay those who deserve it," says the Lord' (Romans 12:19).

That is easy to do when you know the person didn't really mean to hurt you or if it was a small matter that hardly affected you; but when it's big and inflicts severe damage, then what? My childhood was stolen, and nothing my father could do could bring that back. I wanted to let go of the past – but forgive? It was too hard. On the one hand I hated all the feelings that controlled me, I wanted to be rid of them; but how?

The first thing I faced was my anger. I couldn't let go of my past until I let my anger out. Some people thought they were being helpful when they told me I should forgive and forget. They made it sound so easy, like flicking on a light switch. I thought they were being insensitive in expecting me suddenly to emerge from a lifetime of abuse. I think it is wrong to impose on someone that they must forgive. In my experience, forgiveness is a process; it can take time. It is an act of the will, but the will has to be coaxed into taking the right action!

If I hadn't dealt with my anger, it would still be there eating away at me. And I have learnt that anger can very easily turn into bitterness. Bitterness means that you will never be able to let go or move on. With bitterness inside, the enemy will always have control; it is like a poison that gradually stifles the whole body, mind and spirit, and prevents new growth and restoration. I had to mourn the loss of my childhood. Having never experienced a 'normal' childhood, I have never been quite sure what that meant. I did try. But it was too painful, so I closed that part down. God asks us to say we are sorry and then he will forgive us. My father has never asked me to forgive him concerning the abuse, so how could I do it?

'If you forgive those who sin against you, your heavenly Father will forgive you. But if you refuse to forgive others, your Father will not forgive your sins.' These verses (Matthew 6:14–15) always annoyed me and seemed unjust. It makes sense, but to me at that time things were not that easy. So I started to pray that God would help me 'let go'; and that's when things started to move forward. I couldn't forgive but I was now willing to move towards forgiving; I wanted to be able to forgive. That was a real turning point for me. I knew what the Bible said, and with my willingness to try and get there I knew God would help me.

During times at church or when talking to Christians, I would often hear a phrase being mentioned: 'Put it at the foot of the cross and leave it there', or 'Take it to the cross'. What were they on about?

Asking God to take it away was a favourite prayer for me, but he never took it all away. That healing never came. Why? Was I not praying correctly? Was God ignoring my prayer? Was I refusing to let go?

Looking back, I realise now that I was using prayer as a cop-out. I wanted God to do all the work and for me to feel better. But that's not the way God works; at least not for me! I had to meet him halfway. I did notice that I had less violent mood swings and fewer incidents would trigger memories and stir up those familiar feelings of anger. So God was helping me slowly. I felt as though every time I opened up and addressed the issue and faced it honestly, God would take that small piece away and replace it with his love. It has taken me a long time to recognise this and understand why I couldn't get a quick fix.

I've since had it explained to me that because my experience of sexual abuse started at a young age, as most abuse cases do, and because I was abused frequently and for a long time, my identity had got caught up with it. I was not the person I could have been if I had had different parents. My entire experience consisted of being a girl who had to stay quiet and keep dark secrets. I was a girl who was emotionally damaged, who felt nobody could be trusted and nobody could help. I knew in my head that God could help me, but at first I was scared of the pain I might have to go through. If God had taken all the garbage away in one operation, I would have been left with a gaping hole. Yes, God could fill that, but the shock would have been traumatic and I had already been through enough traumas. I would have panicked if it had all gone at once. Who would I be? If there was no pain involved, what would I learn? What would I do with the new me? There would have been a sense of loss, which sounds strange. But the pain I had was familiar and made me feel secure, which is hard for me to admit now. It's strange, isn't it, that sometimes we cling to the familiar just because it is familiar, however awful it might be, because we are afraid of embracing something new.

When I started to eat again and I no longer had anorexia, I knew I could eat and I would be fine. However, a part of me was so used to not eating, or purging when full, that my instinct was still to avoid food. For a while after I started eating 'normally' again, I could still panic when I looked at food and daily I would have to make myself eat. The healing was gradual, and I felt comfortable with that. Bit by bit I was emerging from wrong eating habits. So I hate to think what would have happened if God had taken all the painful memories of the abuse away overnight. I wouldn't have known how I should be reacting in situations or what the new me should do.

So God was doing his work at a speed which suited me. At this stage, when asked I would say I had forgiven my father ninety per cent. I was too scared to answer a straight 'yes'. I wasn't sure. I was of the understanding that if I put my baggage 'at the cross' I had to leave it there and not go back. I knew I was further down the road and that my life had turned around, but from time to time part of me was worried about what I would find if I went back along that road. Sometimes I had to retrace my steps to check that it was all still there, where I left it. It was. The danger was that I might have picked it all up and brought it back with me.

Now that I am more aware of my feelings and understand them a little better, I can say I have let go of my anger towards my father for what he has done and for what he may still do; I will have to deal with that if and when it happens. As I write these words, I am free from the anger, but there is still a lot of pain.

And so the process begins again. As I face up to the pain, I allow God to take it away piece by piece and replace it with himself. So even though I am still going through the process of healing, I can confidently say that, in time, my identity will no longer be in the abuse. I am moving from being a victim to being a survivor.

20

Healing comes in stages

If I was going to move on I had to face up to the issues that were holding me back. With the help of some good friends and God, I identified my big hang-ups. They were men, God, trusting other people, trusting myself and commitment. All seemed insurmountable. They all seemed impossible to change. For many years I had decided to work round them and find my own way through life by avoiding these contentious challenges.

I would say that the first part of my healing began the day I met Cam. We do believe that God brought us together even though we didn't know him then. God wasn't even in our thoughts on the night we got together in Cruze, that gay bar in Manchester. It's such an unlikely story, and an even more surprising coming together of two people who for all intents and purposes would not normally have met. Cam was into the club scene whereas I was into the whole Goth scene – we could not have been more different! I had long dark purple hair and wore black clothing. I fancied guys who were a bit different; I liked them to have long hair, to be wearing leather clothes and make-up. I liked depressing and aggressive music. But Cam had short hair and was into this repetitive beat music. We were at opposite ends of the spectrum!

I think my healing started with Cam because he had a different attitude towards me; nobody had ever treated me in the way Cam treated me. I felt, right from the start, that he respected me and believed in me. He thought I was special. He always said that he loved me so much – even more than I loved him. And he was right; he did love me more than I loved him. It wasn't that I didn't love him. I did. I loved him more than anybody else I'd met; he really mattered to me, and I genuinely cared about him and didn't want to lose him. But in those early days of our friendship, although I loved him I couldn't love him any more than I did because I couldn't give all of me to him straight away. I was scared.

After Cam, the next major challenge I faced was God; could I really trust him and could he really help me? For me, it was a moment of revelation when I finally realised that I didn't have to become a 'better person' before he would love me, that he loved me just as I was. Before this I had the idea that I had to do something to earn his love. But of course this was wrong thinking and it was with sheer relief that I understood that Jesus was my friend and would help me along the road towards healing and finding a new life. So then I felt accepted by two people, God and Cam.

Then meeting people at our church helped me: people like Angie, Roger, Helen and Steve. They seemed to accept me no matter how much I tried to shock them or push them away. And I really did try to shock them in those early days! I suppose it was my way of finding out how genuine they were. But their quiet sincerity and their patience and love won the day and gradually, as I began to change, they were there for me. They never once pointed the finger at me or told me I had to do this or do that. How easily they could have given up on me then.

Getting to know the Tribe and everyone involved with them

helped, as I met people who had struggled with issues in their lives and they were telling me how God had helped them. This made me realise that I wasn't the only one to have major problems – some of these folk had harrowing stories to tell, too. To see and hear that they really believed in God impressed me. When they stood on stage and told their stories to the kids listening, it was clear to me that they were all trying to live what they preached; there was nothing two-faced about them. It was encouraging to hear that none of their lives were straightforward, not even Andy and Michele Hawthorne's. And I was impressed that they were prepared to share their stories and their shame so publicly. These people were so delighted to have found God that they couldn't keep quiet about it! They were so happy.

My wedding was healing to me because I realised I had got to the point of trusting another man implicitly for the first time in my life.

When I gave birth to Romani I was so surprised that I had a girl. Surely I would have a boy! But the Lord had other ideas. It was as if he was saying, 'Trust me.' I did and I can honestly say that I have never been suspicious of Cam's relationship with our daughters at all. He is a wonderful father to them and I have never been nervous of leaving him alone with them. Seeing Romani growing up is fantastic, and now with Teaha, our second daughter, I am doubly thrilled. Occasionally it saddens me to see how happy they are when I can't remember being like that as a little girl; but those moments are short-lived and I am really enjoying sharing their childhood. I play games with them and become like a child again with them. God is restoring what the locusts have stolen. He is healing me through Romani and Teaha. I now know in my heart that the curse has been broken and I don't have to live like I used to.

Life has been a series of ups and downs for a long time. I would make progress and be healed of something, then the doubts would start to whisper to me again. I remember the time when I realised that I didn't need to win my parents' approval any more. Just as I began to enjoy the freedom that this realisation brought, in my head I would hear a voice saying, 'But you live in a rough part of Manchester, what would your parents think? This is not what you were born for. This is not good enough for you.' And then a battle would start inside my mind. 'This is not what my parents would want for me. They would want me to live in a big house with a rich man. They would like me to be visiting them with the grandchildren and everyone being polite to each other.' But no, that is not what I wanted. I came from a place of materialism and outward respectability but underneath it was all false. There is no respectability in abuse or being afraid to say anything in case the peace was broken. I may live in a small ex-council house with a small garden. We may only have one car. My children will be going to the local school. But I am happy. I owe nothing and I have a happy, loving, honest family. I may want for some things but I don't need anything. This has been a big healing to me. I always said that I wouldn't ever buy a council house or send my children to the local school. I was a snob, just like my father.

About one month before the court case I went to Maranatha for a session of 'life' prayer. It was suggested to me by a friend who thought it would help me to come to terms with the past in preparation for the gruelling time that the trial would inevitably be. She was obviously aware that the memories the trial would stir could be painful. So I found myself sat in a room with three other people – they were going to pray through my life with me; two of them I had never met before and they knew nothing about me. The four of us began by praising God and praying.

We are commanded to give praise and thanks and so we did. They told me it was important for me to join in with the prayer at all times and through all stages of the life prayer.

And so we continued. I wasn't sure what to expect and felt

slightly apprehensive, but also very positive about what might happen after this time of prayer. I was asked to thank God for my creation, then to thank him for my ancestors and my bloodline. This was amazing because one of the women asked if I had foreign blood in the family. Yes I did; we had connections with South Africa and my granny has Danish blood in her family.

I was asked to give thanks for my parents. This was hard; at this stage I felt alone. I felt deserted by my mother. It took me a long time to give thanks for them. I cried a lot. At first I just couldn't get the words out, there was so much pain inside. I could feel my stomach in knots. Why should I thank God for them anyway? But when I did, I felt relief. It was important that I didn't just pretend to give thanks for them, I had to want to do it and then mean it.

The next thing was to thank the Lord for my life. This too was hard. I started to cry again and get angry. Why should I thank him for my life? All I could think about was the pain.

Then it was suggested I thanked God for my conception. One of the other women said she could sense that it was not a happy conception or pregnancy that my mother had with me. She was right. My mother didn't tell anyone in her family that she was pregnant with me until the November, and I was born in the January. I felt unwanted and unloved during this part of the prayer time. I kept on focusing on Psalm 139, that God knew me before I was knitted together. 'You made all the delicate, inner parts of my body and knit me together in my mother's womb. Thank you for making me so wonderfully complex! Your workmanship is marvellous – and how well I know it' (Psalm 139:13–14).

Then I had to give thanks for my childhood. Well, what was there to say? Again I was in tears and in pain. I was asked to think of the good things. There weren't many happy memories that I could think of. There probably were some, but the abuse overshadowed them. I gave thanks for my grandparents and times with Elspeth and my extended family on my mother's side. This was the worst moment of the prayer time; I felt the terror again and feelings of isolation.

I found giving thanks for my adult life was easier. I focused on Romani and Cam and what God had done in my life.

The last thing I was encouraged to give thanks for was the relationships with people that God had placed along the way to show me he was looking out for me and also to show me that humanity was not all evil. I wasn't sure what they meant at first, but one of the women asked me about a female at primary school who left while I was there, but whom I got on well with. This was Miss Limvsey. She was my teacher around the age of seven. I got on well with her. She was my favourite teacher, but she got married and left to live in America. I really missed her. Then there was Mr Wilkinson, who taught me when I was eleven. I thought of him as a friend. The woman asked about male friendships and instantly I thought of Richard Waddington, a boy from Rickerby – I remembered how well we got on – and also Phil. I still think of him as a close friend even though we have not seen each other for seven years. I have recently got in contact with him again. We never saw each other that often, usually once a year, but when I lived in Melrose I bumped into him at a time when I really needed a friend. Even though we didn't see each other that often, we could always pick up where we left off. He was a real soul mate.

After all these prayers we went upstairs to another prayer room where I lay down on my back. The three women prayed over my eyes, that I would be healed from all the evil that I had seen. Then they prayed over my ears, that I would be healed of all the lies I had heard and sounds that had upset me. Then my nose and lips, that God would heal me from the effects and the memories of all the smells and tastes that would remind me of the past. They prayed over my mind, to be healed from the effects of the past; and finally they prayed over my whole body. When they had finished I felt relaxed yet refreshed. I left there believing I was healed. It was an important and significant help in coping with the trauma of the court case and walking into the 'battle' against my parents.

I have come to appreciate the power of prayer. It is immediate. We can pray at any time and in any place. God is always there listening to our prayers. We do not have to use special language. God prefers it if we are just ourselves. I left Maranatha knowing that the prayers I had prayed that day, and the prayers that the others had prayed on my behalf, had been answered. It would just be a matter of time before I saw the answers in reality.

21

Never give up giving up

If there is one thing I have learnt about coming through the experience of being sexually abused it is to expect everything when praying for healing, but not to feel disappointed if you do not receive your healing all at once. As I have already described earlier in this book, if God had healed me in an instant I would not have known who I was! I would have had an identity crisis. After all, I was the product of years of pain and trouble that had shaped my life and my reactions, my outlook and my attitudes. And at times I was a very angry person! I can remember reading about Job in the Bible, and how he got very angry with God, blaming him for everything that had gone wrong in his life; but I also noticed that God never reprimanded Job.

And so it was for me; I think God encouraged me to go into partnership with him so that we could work together in exploring and entering the wonderful new life that he has given me today. Together we have tackled the pain, but not before I was prepared to give it all up. And together we tackled the anger, when I was ready to let it go. God never threatened me.

He never manipulated me. He was always there for me and I quickly learnt that he wanted the best for me. He is very patient with me – far more patient with me than I am with myself! He has sometimes waited a long time for me to be ready to work with him; but waited he has, and I am very grateful to him for this.

Over the past few years, I have gradually learnt that it's quite normal to feel angry or sad or rejected. After all, we get hurt because we are people with feelings; but it seems to me that it's what we do with our feelings that is important! I have learnt that if these negative feelings are buried they will just keep coming back. So if we feel angry we will give out anger. Our words and attitudes reflect our emotions. Whatever we think, we are. Our minds control our thoughts, so the Bible says, 'We must renew our minds', which in my experience is a daily task. The Apostle Paul put it this way in the letter he wrote to the Romans, 'Don't copy the behaviour and customs of this world, but let God transform you into a new person by changing the way you think' (Romans 12:2). So I may feel a certain way but I have a choice in what I do with those feelings. I can make a conscious decision to think about something else or I can choose to dwell on those thoughts and entertain them a little longer.

As I explored these things, I gradually came to see that if I changed my thoughts then my feelings changed and no longer seemed to rule my life. I have found that confronting my fears and emotions can be very hard, and the temptation is always to give up and just wallow in hopelessness. But, if my experience is anything to go by, we can cause more problems for ourselves by avoiding them. We can convince ourselves that we don't have a big problem (denial), but if we do that we can end up with an even bigger problem than the one we started with.

The most helpful way I have found of coping with these emotional issues is to find a safe environment in which to explore ourselves, and with God beside us all things become possible!

Sometimes I find prayer difficult; in fact, I often do! I have found that if I cannot pray then I try and worship God instead. In worship many things happen: most important of all, when we are worshipping God we automatically take our eyes away from our problems and focus our gaze on Jesus. There we find a friend who will help us. Worship is another way to connect with God. When we worship we are giving something to him. But the remarkable thing I have learnt is that I can never outgive God; when I give myself to him in worship, I always find that he gives me back so much more!

For a long time I thought that God might help other people, but that he certainly wouldn't want to help me. But then I came to realise that I was wrong in taking that line of thinking, because when I was reading the Bible one day I discovered some verses that say, 'If God is for us who can be against us?' (Romans 8:31).

So gradually I came to realise that God offers everybody help and a new life; but we can't just add it on to the end of our old life with all its experiences, we must sort out the old life first. In my experience this is a process, and we have to face up to what has happened to us. Then, the Bible says that God chooses to forget our sins: 'I will never again remember their sins and lawless deeds' (Hebrews 10:17). But, as human beings, we find we cannot easily forget our past experiences, so we have to continue until we reach the point where we find peace about what has happened to us. If, like me, you were abused, remember it was not your fault. The abuser is the one with the problem; it was their choice to behave in that way, not yours.

The other thing I have come to realise is that it is never too late to let God into those memories that cause us so much pain. I carried too much for too long on my own. In fact, I became used to living with our little secret. But the longer I carried the secret, the harder life became. I realise that this is easy to say, but if we don't start letting God deal with all that has gone wrong with our lives, then what is the alternative?

As you will have gathered from the story so far, it took me a while to fully accept that God is my heavenly Father. But then, as the truth dawned on me, I realised that if God is my true Father and he is truly perfect, then how much does he want to help and restore me? Another verse in the Bible helped me to understand this; I found this in the letter of Paul to the Ephesians and it really encouraged me: 'His unchanging plan has always been to adopt us into his own family' (Ephesians 1:5).

Then another verse completed the picture for me: 'So you should not be like cowering, fearful slaves. You should behave instead like God's very own children, adopted into his family – calling him "Father, dear Father" ' (Romans 8:15).

So I was making progress slowly. But there was one person I really wanted to talk to, and that was my mother. I so wanted to ask her why she had turned her back on me during the court case. No matter how much I prayed about this or talked to people who understood how I felt, I couldn't let this question go; it kept coming back to haunt me.

Then the breakthrough came, just as this book was about to go to the printers in May 2001.

One Saturday afternoon, the phone rang. It was my granny, telling me that my mother was dying. At best, she only had until Christmas to live – just seven months.

This news came as a shock but not a surprise. My whole life, as part of this family, has been a series of twists and turns. Nothing has ever been straightforward; there has always been something happening. In fact, if nothing untoward was happening then I would be waiting for the next drama to emerge – such was the tension I had become so used to living with. I had come to the conclusion that if ever my mother and I were to get on talking terms again, then something tragic would have to happen to one of us – and now this had happened to my mother and I only had, at the most, seven months to be with her.

The next day, as I wondered what to do, I walked around feeling numb for hours on end. I wanted to cry, but the tears wouldn't fall. I think I was in shock. But later that evening I decided that I would visit her – I would set off the following morning.

So, on the Monday morning, I travelled up to see my mother, taking my daughters Romani and Teaha with me. I wondered how she would react at seeing me again after so long. And I wondered further how she would react towards her two grandchildren, whom she had never met.

We arrived. I parked the car outside her house and knocked on her door. She was pleased to see us; we had a great response from her and in a way it seemed as if nothing had ever happened. Bizarre! One moment we would be like a happy family again; the next moment I would remember why I hadn't spoken to her for a very long time; and the moment after that, I would remember that she was dying. My emotions were all over the place. Looking back, I find it difficult to remember how I felt at seeing her again that day. But the girls loved her, as I expected they would; they are still young enough to accept situations as they find them.

And it was good to watch my mother being a grandmother; she seemed to be happy to meet Romani and Teaha. Romani called her 'Mummy's mummy' to start with, and then called her 'Granny' after that. From time to time, my mother would appear to check herself and momentarily withdraw into her thoughts and become hesitant with us all. I think she was trying to be careful to say the right thing so we would not fall out again.

My mind was working overtime to understand what was going on. I had so many questions I wanted to ask. I remembered what I'd been taught on my counselling course and it helped me to accept my mother for who she was. Recently, I have learnt to value people for who they are and not what they may or may not have done. I now realise that my mother is a human being and not a perfect mother, as I had always wanted her to be. So my thinking had changed and matured to the point where, when I looked at my mother, I viewed her almost as an equal and not up on a pedestal or as someone who has to be revered.

On the next day, Tuesday, it seemed strange still being with my mother in her house, but also OK. I wasn't sure if that was because I had dealt with a lot of the past already or if it was God answering the prayers of everyone back home in Manchester. Being with my mother for those few days showed me that I have dealt with a lot over the past few years.

We talked about my father a bit. My mum told me that he had received notice that she was divorcing him. Apparently his reaction was, 'Can you not postpone it?' My father has never lived in reality. Before my mother was diagnosed with cancer, she told me that he often phoned and wrote to her. But since he'd heard about her illness he had only been in touch once, to say he could not sleep at night.

I felt relieved that I had made the decision years ago to leave my family's money and 'status' well alone. And I am very happy. If Cam and I were to lose our house and what little money we have I know that I would still be happy. As I said before, I may want for things but I have no need for things. I have God, Cam and my daughters and now my mother back for a while. What else is there? Needs and wants are not the same thing to me any more.

On the Wednesday we left. I knew I would be back again soon. Cam asked me in the car, 'How do you feel?' I couldn't answer; I was still not sure.

On the Thursday I went to see my counsellor, and he was great. He explained to me the process of loss and grief. Even though my mother was not dead, I was still experiencing a sense of bereavement. I was in shock and feeling numb. I remember not being able to function very well. The house was a tip and I had no motivation to tidy it up. There was little food in the cupboards and I couldn't face shopping. Friends would phone but I couldn't hold a full conversation with them. It was as though my mind had shut down. I could feel a massive weight on top of me. I would watch the TV and not be able to concentrate; it was as if I could just hear noise. I felt exhausted all the time. I simply wanted to go to bed and sleep. I was there in body but not in mind.

I was due to go to college that night as part of my training to be a counsellor. That particular night we were being taught how to counsel a client who was dealing with loss, grief or bereavement. It's just as well we were given handouts as I don't think I retained much of the lesson. One thing I do remember, though, was that we were asked to write down any losses we had experienced throughout our lives. The loss could have been an item or person or pet. When I wrote my losses down I realised that there were many; I also realised I still had a lot to deal with!

22

More surprises

I had been invited to Lindz's wedding the following Saturday (he is in the Tribe), but with the events of the past few days still swirling around in my thoughts I could not bring myself to go. I didn't want to see everyone and have them all asking me, 'How are you?' I knew that they had been praying for my mother and me as we were reunited, but even so I could not face it. I wouldn't have felt comfortable. So Cam and I had a quiet weekend. By Friday night I felt the weight of the situation lift, which enabled me to function a little better. So I tidied the house and started to eat again. Cam asked me whether I was better or just in denial. Partly denial, I think.

I was keen to go back to Scotland and see my mother, and it so happened that a few days later Cam had a meeting in Carlisle. So the children and I went with him, dropped him off and continued to my mother's house. I was grateful that she now lives in a new house which she bought about a year ago; this meant I didn't have to go back to Luce where the abuse happened – I'm not sure how I would have reacted going back there, especially with my own little girls.

However, even though my mother is in a different house, it is still a little strange going there because one room in particular contains a lot of furniture that was in the old house. In fact, the way she has positioned the furniture is almost a copy of the front room in which we confronted my father before the trial. On one wall is a picture of Luce House. At first I wondered why she would want to be reminded of that place; but then I realised that when she looks at it she remembers good times, whereas I can't look at it without feelings of revulsion.

Sometimes I want her to feel how I feel, but we are different people with different memories.

That night an old friend came to visit me. She had stayed in touch with my mother whereas I had lost contact with her years ago. I knew my mother still saw her but I never contacted her because I didn't want to turn her against my mother. This might not have happened, but I was unsure what my mother had told her. What version of events did she know, I wondered.

But it was great seeing her again. We used to hang around with each other when we were about eleven years old and remained good friends until she got married. After that we lost touch with each other.

After we'd been chatting for a while, our conversation turned to the trial and I asked her what she thought when she'd read the reports of the trial in the papers. She replied that she'd been shocked but not surprised. Most people I talk to say that, so at first I didn't question her further. But something made me return to the subject later; maybe it was the way she looked when she mentioned my father. Anyway, later on I asked her why she hadn't been surprised at the outcome of the court case. She told me that one night she had stayed at Luce when my parents were having a party. She was in my room sitting on my couch when my father came in and started chatting to her. She told me how he leaned over and touched her breasts. Afterwards she thought to herself that she must have imagined

192

it, or thought he'd just had too much to drink and was being over-amorous. She didn't say a word to anyone about that incident. But when she saw the papers she realised that she hadn't imagined it. What's more, she knew that everything else must be true.

I wasn't shocked, but now I'm left wondering how many others he tried it on with; I don't suppose we'll ever know.

Later that night, after my friend had left, my mother and I sat up chatting. It was nice but I kept finding myself forgetting the past and forgetting that she was dying. Part of me was still holding on to the fact that she needed to get more tests done at the hospital to ascertain exactly how ill she was. I told her that I thought I was in denial – that somehow the doctors would find out that it wasn't as bad as they originally thought.

We talked a lot about counselling, as she is having therapy too. I can see the change in her. I don't know whether that is down to time, therapy, answered prayer or because she knows she hasn't long to live, but she seems to me to be more open compared to when we last met. As I looked at her, I remembered how so many times I had wanted to pick up the phone and speak to her, but I couldn't – I wouldn't have known what to say to the rest of the family if I had. I would have felt disloyal to them, especially after everything we had been through together.

As this book draws to a conclusion, I have just returned from another trip to see my mother with Romani and Teaha. I was feeling OK but really tired and drained emotionally. My head was telling me, 'Remember she has more tests to have; maybe the doctors can do something for her.' At that moment she was on a course of pills, but nothing more.

When we arrived, I thought she looked tired. Her spirits were up as much as can be expected but she looked exhausted. She wasn't eating well as she had lost her appetite and was passing a lot of blood. She sounded tired as well. Romani and

Teaha ran to her as if they had known her all their lives. It was great having them there because they broke up the day. They provided a welcome focus. Romani is three and Teaha is one year old, which meant that they were into everything, and drawing on the carpet instead of paper! A new house and new surroundings are all very exciting for them. So I spent most of that first day following their every movement and moving objects out of arm's reach! If Mum and I started a conversation about the past we rarely finished it; but this helped us avoid the big questions, so we had little reason for ill-feeling between us and it helped me not to dwell on the fact she wasn't going to be here for much longer.

Once the children were in bed we would sit and talk over the past or what my father was saying now. I had so many questions but I was finding it hard to ask them. I didn't want my mother to think that this was all I wanted to talk about, but I had such a need to ask and I knew this opportunity was now or never.

I asked her what it was like living with my father. She told me about a time at Haddington Place, their first house. She was planning to visit my Aunt Elspeth, and the night before she was going my father handed her an envelope and then went out himself. She opened it and found a note inside with a list of household duties she had to take care of before she left in the morning. The list comprised ironing, washing the floors, sorting out his meals for while she was away, etc. She said that it was written in a regimented fashion and she knew she had to do the tasks he had commanded her to do. I asked her what she had thought of his behaviour. She felt that she had no option and just had to do it; therefore she accepted the situation, and so a precedent was set very early in their marriage.

Hearing this reminded me of a session I had had with my counsellor about four months previously. I was telling him how frustrated I felt that when Cam went out, he just went, whereas when I wanted to go out I thought that I had to make sure the children had everything they needed – the bottles made up, lunches ready, Cam's lunch ready, the house clean and everything left just so. I would make sure that Cam would have no hassle and that it would be easy for him and the kids. My counsellor asked me why I did this. I told him I felt that I had to. He asked me whether Cam demanded this and what would be the worst thing that could happen if I walked out, as Cam did, and left them to it. I thought – nothing! Cam would find what he needed and the girls would be fine. It dawned on me then that I had seen my mother do this and I was automatically doing the same. I was shocked, because I was not aware of this similar pattern of behaviour at all. I thought I was so different from my mother. The worst thing was that I was actually laying down the same behavioural patterns for the girls. So I decided to change. It was like a revelation. Now I had recognised the situation, I had a choice; I could carry on in the same way or do something about it.

So I did do something about it. These days when I go out and leave Cam with the girls I make sure there are food and nappies in the house – but he has to do the finding and the preparation now. This way the girls will be able to see that Mummy doesn't do everything and that Daddy can do everything that Mummy does. Cam and I have more of an equal balance now around the house, and I believe this can only be a good thing for all of us.

I feel that most of the family are at a place where their pain and anger have lessened. I know that Elspeth and I can accept my mother now. We both believe that she did what she thought was right and what she had to do to survive. I was angry that she didn't leave my father before the trial, but she explained that things were not that straightforward. He had run up a lot of debt and had been out of work for two years while pretending to work. They were partners, so the debt was her responsibility too. She told me that she wanted to clear her name and it also gave her something else, other than the trial, to focus on. She knows that she could have stayed with any member of the family, but she made the decision to sort things out for herself and, to her credit, she has since managed to clear all of the debt.

She has started divorce proceedings and doesn't want anything else to do with my father. She now accepts what he did to us but still can't believe she chose a man like that to marry. She feels conned.

Today she has a fridge magnet that says,

A friend is someone who understands your past
Believes in your future
And accepts you today the way you are.

I don't understand the past fully but I do believe in the future.

On returning home, I talked to Elspeth. She has been on an Alpha course and attends church as often as she can; her faith grows daily. She struggles with some issues, but don't we all? I see such a change in her. Two years ago she was standing in the waiting room at court, turning her Tarot cards over.

Two weeks ago, in mid-June, my mother received the results of her biopsy. The consultant told her that they could not find the primary source of the cancer but that she had secondary tumours in her bowel and in her liver. The prognosis is not good. She will be having some medication in two weeks' time but there will be side-effects. However, if the medication works she might live a little longer. Writing this makes it all seem a bit more real. It really hasn't sunk in yet . . . I was hoping that the tests would have offered more hope.

I feel that I do not need to question her any more; I don't need answers now. I have accepted the fact that she didn't do things the way I wanted her to, or the way I would have done, but then I am not her. She is a person in her own right and I accept that now. It must have been hard for her, living with my father. My counsellor gave me a scenario: two children are playing in their bedroom when they are told that there is a monster in the wardrobe. They have two choices; one is to open the wardrobe and confront what might be in there, and the alternative is never to open the door. I would open the door and confront it, but that's only because I've changed and grown over the years away from my father. I believe if I hadn't moved away I would never have opened the door. I am sure that my mother wouldn't have opened the door either.

When I was talking to my friend, the last time I was up in Scotland, we remembered some of the daft things we got up to. It was great to see her but she also made me start to think about some of the good times I had in my childhood. With her help, I could remember that there were times of happiness; but they usually occurred when my father wasn't around. I had a lot of good times with my mother too. All my friends thought she was great, and I suppose she was. I now want to have a balanced remembrance of my past. When I look back now I want to see the good things more than the bad; I feel that it is nearing the time to put the past to rest for me, even though this is just the start of my ministry to the abused.

Last week a Christian woman with a gift of prophecy was over in the UK from America and I was introduced to her. She came and spoke to Cam and me. I was a little scared of her and expected her to tell me I was a sinner, but she didn't. Even though I'd never met her before, she told me she had something from the Lord for me and started to speak. My friend wrote down what she said.

She started by telling me that the depression I was feeling and had been feeling all my life was going to end, that I had been in oppression and depression since an early age. She said that at the moment things were bad and seemed to be getting worse because my girls were coming to the age of when the trauma towards me started – age four, she told me. When she said 'four' I felt as though I had been run over. She went on to say that it all had been allowed to happen because I was going to speak out – to be a voice for those who can't speak out. She said that she could see me writing. Everything she said was spot on and really encouraging. Since then my spirit has lifted and I have been in a much better place.

I hope my story has encouraged you if you too are a victim of abuse. But for the remainder of this book, I would like to address youth and church leaders as to how they can provide a climate in which people feel free to offload their 'secrets' and become survivors rather than remain victims.

23

For youth workers and church leaders

One of the reasons for telling my story is to help Christians understand how traumatic sexual abuse is for those who have experienced it. The following facts may prove illuminating.

- Not everyone who abuses has been abused.
- Not everyone who has been abused will go on to abuse.
- Not all offenders are men.
- Most women survivors do not abuse their own children.
- Sexual abuse is not necessarily a product of a dysfunctional family.
- Sexual abuse does occur in every area of society – even among Christians.
- Children do not lie about abuse; they have no awareness of sexual activity normally.
- 85 per cent of abusers are *known* to the child.

- 80 per cent of abuse is carried out either in the abuser's home or in the child's home.
- Some mothers do know if their husband/partner is abusing their children.
- When a person is abused it *will* have an effect on them.
- Babies as young as three months old have been abused.
- 38 per cent of girls are sexually abused before the age of eighteen. (This figure comes from *The Secret Trauma* by D. Russell *et al.*, 1986.)
- 16 per cent of boys are sexually abused before the age of eighteen. (From *Sexual Abuse in a National Survey* by D. Finkelhor *et al.*, 1990.)
- Only 5 per cent of cases are reported and only 35 per cent of these lead to charges. (From the Department of Health, 1988.)
- The typical child sex offender molests an average of 117 children, most of whom do not report the offence. (From US National Institute of Mental Health, 1988.)

Whilst these statistics are shocking they clearly do not reflect the true extent of the problem. With 95 per cent of abuse cases not being reported we can only guess at the enormity of the situation. It is so hard to speak out, especially when we consider that 85 per cent of offenders are known to the victim, sometimes even living in the same house. In circumstances like this, how can a child find the courage to speak out? We are raised to respect our elders and the privacy of our family, so whom can children talk to? I believe it is the responsibility of all of us; whether as a parent, sister, brother, aunt, uncle or friend of the family, we all have to make sure that children know they have a place to go where they will be believed and protected.

The National Society for the Prevention of Cruelty to Children has some further disturbing statistics on its web pages. To underline the scale of the problem, results from an

NSPCC survey of twenty-one countries, including Britain, found 36 per cent of women and 29 per cent of men had been abused as children.

EFFECTS OF ABUSE

It was many years before I realised that I was not alone in being abused. Many years of keeping 'our little secret' affected me. Maybe you are reading this book thinking that, until now, nobody else has known about your secret. If that is the case, you will probably be feeling all of the following emotions. If you're reading this book and happily have never experienced the violation of abuse, then this list may help you to understand how we victims can feel.

- Guilt
- Anger
- Fear
- Fear of being on your own at night
- No emotional reactions in certain situations
- Anxiety
- Isolation
- Eating disorders
- Not wanting to be touched
- Self-harming
- Under-achieving
- Promiscuous
- Flashbacks
- Lack of childhood memories
- Nightmares
- Insomnia
- Lack of trust
- Hatred of men/women
- Bad reactions to dental or other intimate medical procedures
- Confusion

- Low self-esteem
- A loner
- Rebellious
- Abuse of drugs, alcohol
- Self-blame
- Parenting issues
- Depression
- Sadness
- Panic attacks
- Reactions to certain smells
- Reactions to certain music

(From *Surviving Child Sexual Abuse* by L. Hall and S. Lloyd, 2nd edition, 1993, Falmer Press)

These are consequences not just of sexual abuse but also of mental abuse or deprivation, or emotional or physical abuse. Because of these effects it can take a long time to turn them around. Some people might have to face each of their struggles individually, whereas others may be able to deal with them all at the same time. There are no set rules.

ADDED DIFFICULTIES FOR CHRISTIANS

Sometimes I have heard Christians who have been abused describe the following difficulties:

- A fear of the Holy Spirit
- A feeling that it is wrong to feel angry
- A fear of intimacy with God and being filled with the Holy Spirit
- Not wanting to take communion when it is placed in their mouths by the priest
- A feeling of the leader being the parent and the congregation being the child
- Not wanting to hug anybody

Figures vary. Some statistics state that 1 in 7 people have been abused before the age of eighteen. Some say that it is 1 in 4. Whatever the number, it is too many and there may well be sufferers in your church. There will be some you know of and others you don't. Some may have peace about it, others may not. There could be abusers in your church as well; this does happen in the Christian world. I want to encourage the church leaders and youth workers to tackle this problem head on and take advantage of the awareness in society at the moment. I believe we have to offer help to anyone who has been involved in abuse, whether as the victim or the perpetrator.

In my Touch Point Bible it says this: 'Love and abuse cannot dwell together. To knowingly hurt someone – physically, mentally, emotionally, sexually – is to declare a lack of love for that person. Acts of abuse drown out all words of love, no matter how sincere they may sound.'

In Romans 13:10 we read: 'Love does no wrong to anyone, so love satisfies all of God's requirements.'

Before you seek out those who have been abused you must have certain vital elements in place.

Have somebody who is prepared to listen and believe what they hear

- The most important factor while listening to abused people is to give them space and time and believe them.
- Most abused people think they will not be believed. Helpers should emphasise the fact that they are there to listen, and that even though it may shock them or be painful, they will still respect and love the person. Most abused people do not disclose graphic details straight away, they usually test the water to see if and how you will respond. When I first disclosed to friends what had happened to me, I always wondered what they were thinking and what they thought of me now.

- Time is important too. I know that some people want to go home after church, but if you are going to tackle this issue you must be prepared that, for people who want to talk, it may take time. It is no good telling them that they are brave for coming forward and then saying you only have ten minutes. I know that when I first started telling people what had happened to me, all I wanted was for them to listen. I certainly didn't want any advice and I certainly didn't want to hear that I had to forgive.
- Do not ask questions or lead the conversation, because questions can be attacking and make the person feel they have to take responsibility or blame someone else.
- Forgiveness shouldn't be the first thing that they are told to do; letting go is more appropriate, and is one of the translations of the Greek word Jesus used for forgiveness.

Have a ministry team ready to pray

- We all know of people who are always going forward for ministry but never seem to get better. Please don't judge: unless you have been there you don't know how hard this issue is.
- I have been dealing with the effects of my experience for four years now, and it is very easy for me to believe that everything is healed only to find myself in tears in church again six months later. We all need to have the ongoing support of a good prayer team.

Have professional help available

- Some people might need to talk over issues with a counsellor. I am seeing one at the moment, a guy who is a professional counsellor and who is also a Christian. We need to be very careful that the help we offer is sound. I believe the wrong counsellor can do more harm than good. In the end it is God who brings the healing, not the counsellor.

Have both men and women listeners available

- Do not expect just women to come forward. It is harder for men to talk about abuse. They have the same issues as women, but for men there is the added pressure of 'will everyone think I am gay?' Not every man who has been abused is gay and not every man who is gay has been abused. Women do not have this problem.

- Think of ways that people can stay anonymous but find help; they may have never disclosed their secret and may still want to keep quiet about it.

- It could be announced in church that the following week there will be a box in the foyer of the church, with an invitation to anyone who has been affected by any kind of abuse to write on a piece of paper what they have done or what kind of abuse they have suffered and put it into the box; no names needed.

- Or have a cross in the foyer with an empty basket below it. Have another basket full of pebbles close by. Ask the same thing, but invite them to place a pebble below the cross. This way you can get an idea of how many people in your church need support, and this way they can stay anonymous if they wish.

- Or if you know of survivors in your church, or other churches you have connections with, you could ask them to write a small article to encourage others, and place this alongside your church's other information.

- Or you could ask your pastor or a visitor to talk about the effects of abuse in your main service. The talk would have to take place in your church to your congregation as a whole. You could not ask vulnerable people to expose themselves by coming to a special talk held on a Saturday or whenever; you have to provide a safe environment for them.

- Or your church could address the issue through drama or other presentations.

SOME OTHER THINGS TO CONSIDER

- Does your church have links with organisations that can help you if abuse is disclosed?
- What would you do if a child in your church disclosed about abuse?
- Would you treat the child differently if the allegation was against a church member?
- Do you have a childcare policy?
- Do you think your church or organisation provides a safe environment for a child to come forward?
- Do you or your youth workers have enough training and support?
- Have you explained to the children you come into contact with the importance of being safe and being able to disclose anything they are worried about to your church/organisation?
- Do you have male and female helpers available?
- Do you have police checks for those who work for you? Police checks are good but are not a hundred per cent safety net. They will only show up those who have been caught.

HURTING PEOPLE IN THE CHURCH

Since I have become a Christian I have met lots of other survivors. Some have come to me to share their stories; others I approached, recognising in their manner that they too had been abused or raped.

Girl A told me that she had just started having memories of abuse and couldn't believe that it had happened. It was because of a close relationship with another male that her mind had been triggered and her memories were coming back. She went for prayer and was told to receive the healing. She thought she had, but two months down the line her pastor mentioned abuse in church and she cracked up. She came to me feeling very down and guilty – guilty because she felt she was not a good Christian. I asked why and she said that if she was a good Christian she should have received the healing God gave her.

Girl B told me that she had gone for prayer about the rape she experienced. She couldn't get over it and kept going back to the helper the church had appointed to her. She was told that it had all been dealt with and that she had to leave it alone now.

Guy A told me about his abuse by a friend of the family and how difficult he found it to have a long-term relationship with anyone, whether a girlfriend or just close friends. He felt that he could not talk to anyone, not even his friends. He was worried that his friends would think of the sexual side of the abuse and wonder whether he was now gay. He felt that the church had nothing to offer him.

Guy B cannot talk about it at all. He won't face what happened to him, although he can talk about his brother's abuse.

Guy C felt that while it was happening to him he could not talk to anyone. His father was a youth leader in their church and liked by everyone. Who would believe him?

We all have a responsibility to help these people.

The key to it all is a willingness to let go.

Useful contacts

CCPAS (The Churches' Child Protection Advisory Service)
P.O. Box 133
Swanley
Kent BR8 7UQ

24-hour helpline: 0845 120 4551
Tel: 0845 120 4550
Website: www.ccpas.co.uk
e-mail: info@ccpas.co.uk

CCPAS advises churches, organisations, child care agencies, children and families on issues of abuse. It offers training for workers and leaders in helping children who might have been abused, and assists churches and organisations in preparing and maintaining child protection policies.

Maranatha Community
102 Irlam Road
Flixton
Manchester M41 6JT

Tel: 0161 748 4858
Website: www.maranathacommunity.org.uk

NSPCC (The National Society for the Prevention of Cruelty to Children)
National Centre
42 Curtain Road
London EC2A 3NH

24-hour helpline: 0808 800 5000
Textphone: 0800 056 0566
Tel: 020 7825 2500
Website: www.nspcc.org.uk

The NSPCC specialises in child protection and the prevention of cruelty to children, and helps children who have suffered cruelty to overcome its effects. The NSPCC helpline is a free and confidential service run by experienced counsellors.

One in Four
219 Bromley Road
Bellingham
London SE6 2PG

Tel: 020 8697 2112
Website: www.oneinfour.org
e-mail: oneinfour@colm.u-net.com

One in Four is an organisation run for and by people who have experienced sexual abuse.

If you would like to be in touch with Tori, you can e-mail her at the following address.
info@ourlittlesecret.org.uk